John Rowlands

Historical notes of the counties of Glamorgan, Carmarthen and Cardigan

and a list of the members of parliament for South Wales, from Henry VIII,

to Charles II

John Rowlands

Historical notes of the counties of Glamorgan, Carmarthen and Cardigan
and a list of the members of parliament for South Wales, from Henry VIII, to Charles II

ISBN/EAN: 9783337266714

Printed in Europe, USA, Canada, Australia, Japan

Cover: Foto ©Andreas Hilbeck / pixelio.de

More available books at **www.hansebooks.com**

THE

CROONIAN LECTURES

FOR 1864,

DELIVERED BEFORE

THE PRESIDENT AND FELLOWS OF THE ROYAL COLLEGE
OF PHYSICIANS OF ENGLAND.

THE SIGNIFICANCE OF DROPSY,

AS A SYMPTOM IN

RENAL, CARDIAC, AND PULMONARY DISEASES.

BY

W. R. BASHAM, M.D.,

FELLOW OF THE COLLEGE; SENIOR PHYSICIAN TO THE WESTMINSTER HOSPITAL; AND
LECTURER ON THE PRINCIPLES AND PRACTICE OF MEDICINE.

LONDON:
JOHN CHURCHILL AND SONS, NEW BURLINGTON STREET.
MDCCCLXIV.

PRINTED BY
J. C. ADLARD, BARTHOLOMEW CLOSE.

TO

THOMAS WATSON, M.D.,

PRESIDENT OF THE ROYAL COLLEGE OF PHYSICIANS OF ENGLAND,
ETC. ETC.

My dear Sir,

Your distinguished position as President of the Royal College of Physicians of England, raised to it as you are by the spontaneous and unanimous voice of the Fellows, would sufficiently justify the dedication of these Lectures to you. But when, to the respect which, in common with all the Fellows of the College, I entertain towards yourself personally, I add the obligation you have laid me under by selecting me to deliver the Croonian Lectures, this dedication becomes the sincere and earnest expression both of my esteem and gratitude. You have afforded me the opportunity of submitting to the College some further observations in connection with forms of disease inseparably associated with the name of one of our most distinguished and lamented Fellows. If these observations are accepted

in the spirit I have offered them, they will lead to further
investigations, and may, perhaps, contribute to the settle-
ment of some doubtful points connected with the pathology
of these diseases.

You, sir, have expressed your approbation of the scope and
object of these Lectures, and I shall ever feel grateful for
the kind attention paid to them by yourself, the fellows,
members, and visitors, as well as for the ready and
cordial assent you gave to my proposal to dedicate them
to you.

I have the honour to be, my dear Sir,

Your very faithful and obedient servant,

W. R. BASHAM.

17, CHESTER STREET, BELGRAVE SQUARE ;
March, 1864.

CONTENTS.

LECTURE I.

LECTURE III.

DESCRIPTION OF THE PLATES.

PLATE I

Represents the general character of the degeneration of tissue in morbus Brightii.

FIG.

1.—Exhibits the granulations on the cortical surface of a kidney; these granulations appear to be formed by the convoluted tubes becoming filled with a granular matter mixed with fat-grains, apparently derived from the breaking up of imperfect and abortive cells. One of the larger straight tubes of Bellini appears filled with fine granular matter and the débris of cells.

2.—Vesical and urethral epithelium, granular and fatty.

3.—Bronchial expectoration in morbus Brightii. The cellular elements do not differ from those seen in the urinary sediment derived from the kidneys, except that a greater variety of modified cells is apparent.

4.—Is a section of a bronchial tube in morbus Brightii. It is typical of the state of those tissues in all cases of renal dropsy. The epithelial cells, as layer after layer come to the surface, never reach the full development of the ciliated epithelial cells, but degenerate into the mucous or pus-corpuscles generated in such abundance.

5, 6.—Are more highly magnified examples of the fatty conditions of the fibro-elastic and unstriped muscular layers.

PLATE II

Represents the degeneration of tissue in the organs of circulation.

1.—Indicates that the milk-spots on the surface of the heart, so often seen in morbus Brightii, result from a degeneration of the serous membrane.

b

FIG.

2.—In every fatal case of morbus Brightii the heart-fibre of either side of the heart will be found characteristic of degeneration.

3.—Opaque patches in the aortic sinus and in the endocardial membrane are very common in morbus Brightii. They are very characteristic of a fatty state of the tissues. Plates of cholesterine mixed with innumerable fat-grains are readily seen with the microscope. 4.—Is a vertical section through one of these opaque patches in the aorta.

5.—Represents the state of the liver cells typical of what is all but universally seen in renal dropsy.

6.—Represents the convoluted tubes of the kidney in chronic morbus Brightii; the epithelial gland-cells are almost everywhere detached from the basement or germinal membrane, and the tubes appear filled with these cells and granular matter and fatty nuclei derived from the breaking up of the most abortive.

PLATES III & IV

Represent the character of the sputa in various pulmonary disorders, with the object of showing that the cellular elements thrown off from the bronchial mucous membrane in various pulmonary disorders, are strictly analogous to what is derived from the renal tubes in diseases of the kidneys.

1.—Represents the hyaline or transparent characters of the sputa in ordinary catarrh. The hyaline and transparent casts in the curable forms of morbus Brightii are strictly analogous. Compare figs. 10, 11, 12, Plate V, in the author's work 'On Dropsy.'

2.—Represents the shreddy fibrinous sputa in plastic bronchitis, similar in character to the fibrinous casts in the earlier stage of acute morbus Brightii. Compare Plate II, fig. 2, of the same work with the above.

3.—The sputa in capillary bronchitis, with characters somewhat similar. The cellular elements are almost identical.

4.—Is the character of the sputa in phthisis. Compare the figure with the sediment of the urine in a case of renal dropsy complicated with cancer or phthisis. See Plate VIII, figs. 1, 2, of the same work.

PLATE IV.

The sputa in pneumonia, of different degrees of intensity, typical of the several forms of casts in the acute form of renal dropsy, particularly those cases which commence with inflammatory engorgement of the kidneys, with evidence of hæmaturia of greater or less degree.

FIG.

1, 2, 3.—Illustrate the milder form, in which the sputa acquire a tinge scarcely deeper than an apricot yellow. It is apparent that this yellow stain arises from certain cells only, large ovoid cells taking up the colouring matter derived from the blood stasis. These cells are those which are sometimes called pigment-cells, from their acquiring and giving to the sputa in bronchial catarrh the steel-gray colour so familiar to us. The ciliated epithelial cells which are first thrown off do not appear stained, nor even the mucous corpuscles.

4, 5.—Represent the sputa in the severer forms of pneumonia, when they become viscid and rust-coloured, or even more deeply tinged. Here all the cells appear more or less stained, as, from the presence of blood-corpuscles, a greater abundance of hæmatin is poured out. The scaly epithelium from the mouth and cheeks is usually free from colour. These forms of sputa have their analogue in the blood-casts of the earliest stage of acute morbus Brightii. The cellular elements are similar in each, and may be verified by examining the urinary sediment in the blood-stained urine after scarlet fever. See Plates I and II, and figs. 1, 2, &c. &c., in the work already quoted.

PLATE V

Represents the character of the changes which take place in the morbid deposits in the heart and arteries.

1.—Represents the starlike character of an opaque earthy spot on the mitral valve of a case mentioned in the text.

2.—Is an opaque spot in the aorta which had undergone the process of calcification; digestion in dilute-hydrochloric acid dissolved the deposit and

FIG.

left the tissue clear. The earthy material is composed of phosphate and carbonate of lime.

3.—Is a deposit of a similar character and composition occurring in a branch of the middle cerebral artery, leading to an apoplectic clot. The rupture of the vessel appeared to have arisen from the loss of elasticity in the coats of the vessel in consequence of the calcification of the tissues.

4, 5, 6.—Are illustrations of the other form of degeneration which the morbid deposit may undergo, leading to dilatation of the cavities and imperfect driving power in the force of the heart.

PLATE VI

Represents the fatty decay of the tissues observed in cases of emphysema and chronic bronchitis terminating in dropsy.

1.—Is a portion of the vesicular structure of an emphysematous lung, showing the numerous fat-grains deposited in it.

2.—Represents sections of the bronchial mucous membrane, showing the successive layers of cells degenerating as they approach the free surface, to be thrown off as mucous and pus-corpuscles mixed with large granule-cells and aggregations of disintegrated nuclei represented in figs. 3, and 4.

5.—Illustrates the fatty condition of the coats of a small artery leading to an emphysematous patch.

6.—Represents a state of fatty degeneration of the muscular fibre of both auricle and ventricle of the right side, and is typical of what may be seen in most cases of dropsy with dilatation of the right cavities, complicated with emphysema and chronic bronchitis.

Fig. 1

Fig. 2.

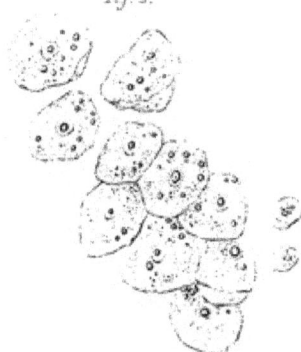

a. *Convoluted tubes, filled with fat granules and granular matter.*
b. *straight tube, filled with debris of cells, &c.*
c. *Glugers or hæmatuary corpuscles*

Vesical & urethral epithelium, granular & fatty.

Fig 3.

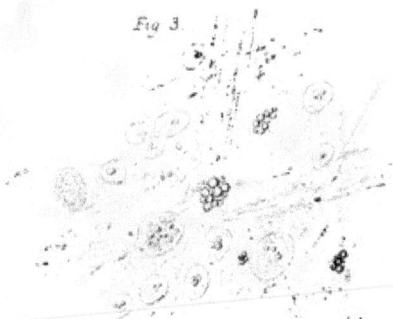

Bronchial expectoration.

Fig 4.

Section of a small bronchial tube.
a. *Layer of epithelial cells.*
b. *Germinal or basement membrane*
c. *Layer of fibro elastic tissue.*
2. *Layer of unstriped musc 3.*

Fig. 5.

Layer of unstriped bronchial tube cells in general 2. slightly fatty. + 350.

Fig. 6.

Layer of unstriped muscle, also fatty, more highly magnified. + 350.

From substance of left ventricle.

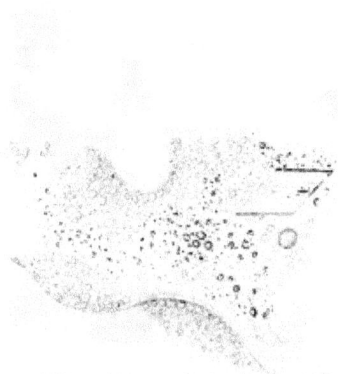

Bacula albida.
Tran. spot from endocardium

From vesicle...

Fig. 3

From opaque spot in aorta.

Fig. 4

Inner serous coat

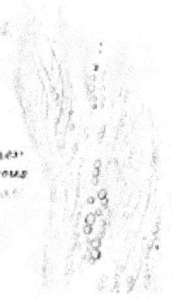

Plate Em 1799
microscopic view of the small town

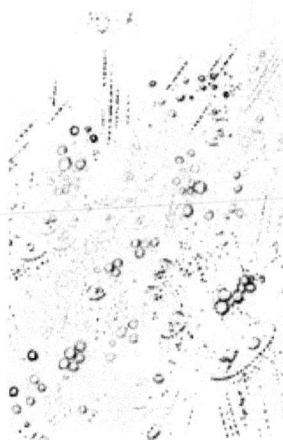
Fig. 4

Plate 4.

Sputa. Pneumonia.

Plate 4.

Fig. 1.

Fig. 2.

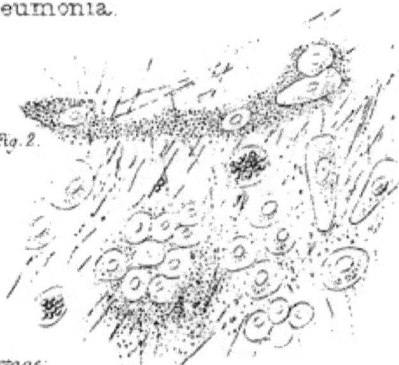

Mild type : early stage.

Fig. 3.

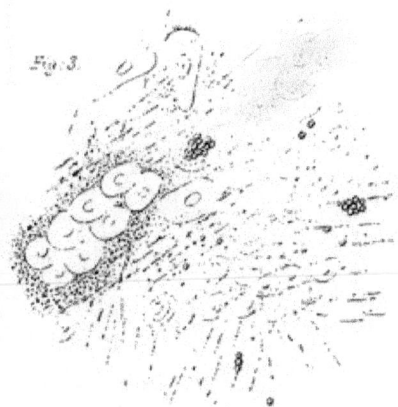

Fig. 4.

Sputa viscid ; yellow tinge.

Sputa viscid ; rust coloured.

Fig. 5.

Fig. 6.

Sputa viscid, n very decidy coloured.

Sputa more purulent.

opaque spot on
; sinus. +350.

digestion in Hydrochloric acid.

An opaque spot on the mitral v
+350.

Fig 3.

small branch of the
die cardinal
...

The same
more highly
magnified.
+350.

Fig 4.

Fig. 1.

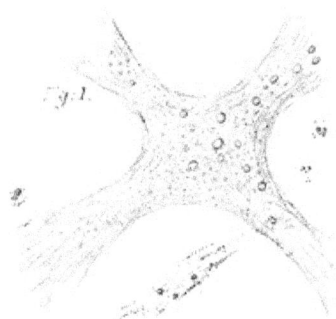

Pulmonary tissue from emphysematous lung.

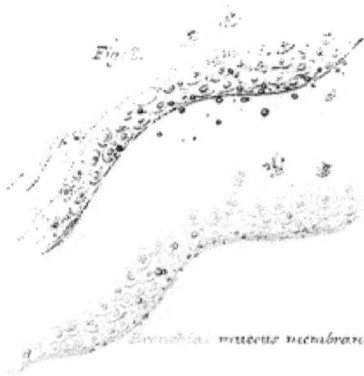

Fig. 2.

Bronchial mucous membrane

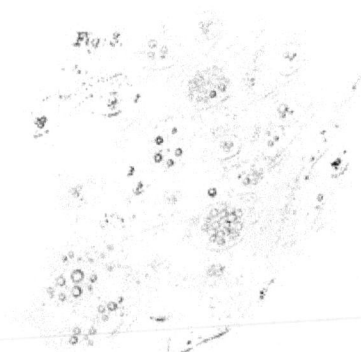

Fig. 3.

Sputa : Chronic Bronchitis with Dropsy.

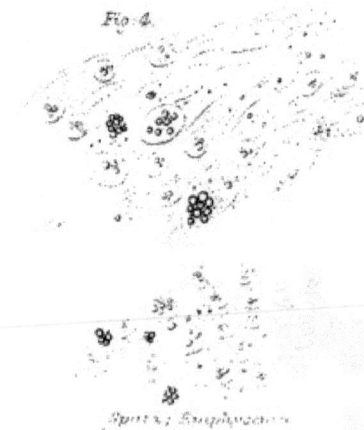

Fig. 4.

Sputa ; Emphysema

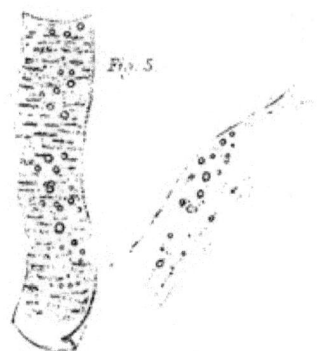

Fig. 5.

Fatty condition of small veins, situated in emphysematous patch.

Fig. 6.

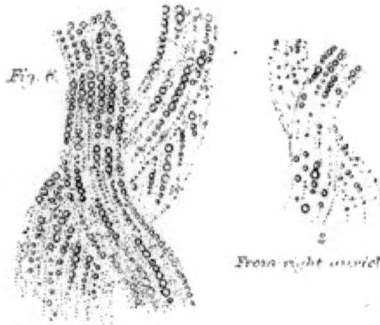

From right ventricle.
Heart fibres.

From right auricle

CROONIAN LECTURES.

THE SIGNIFICANCE OF DROPSY.

LECTURE I.

MR. PRESIDENT AND GENTLEMEN,—In the following lectures I am desirous of inquiring, not so much whether the ancient views and theories of dropsy were right or wrong; not whether their remedies and methods of treatment were appropriate and efficient; but whether our modern methods of investigation by microscopic research are calculated to obtain for us a wider significance for dropsical diseases than has hitherto been accorded to them; and more especially whether those researches have led, or are likely to lead, to any practical result, by which principles of treatment may be made to rest on more expansive pathological views, and which may be reasonably expected to conduce more effectually to the relief or mitigation of those forms of disease.

There are many advantages to be found in selecting a symptom common to several pathological states, and investigating its origin, its progress, and its consequences. Its significance becomes appreciated, and its relation to the favorable or unfavorable progress of the fundamental disease more clearly understood. This proposition is specially applicable to the state which is called Dropsy.

1

It is not long since writers and practitioners viewed
and treated it as a substantive disease. Inattentive to the
true significance of the presence of an accumulated fluid in
the shut cavities, or diffused through the connective tissue
generally, they were content to interpret the presence of
dropsy as arising from one of two causes—either increased
effusion, or diminished absorption ; and regarding the absorbents or veins as alone concerned, these effusions were considered as distinct diseases, and received a place in all noso-
logical systems as special morbid states. Within the last
thirty years we may find writers of distinction discussing the
treatment of the acute, the plethoric, or the arterial dropsy;
advocating bloodletting and remedies to lower the heart's
action in one class of cases; but for dropsies from relaxation,
or glandular obstruction, remedies to stimulate the absorbents
were to be prescribed. Many may remember when such
doctrines prevailed and were taught in our schools.

It is, however, now generally admitted that the absorbents
occupy a less prominent position in the development of
dropsy; and we regard chiefly the state of the capillaries,
especially the venous, and impediments to the free passage of
blood through them, as the most active and intelligible causes
of the transudation of the serous elements of the blood into
the tissues.

Hewson says,* " I think we may be led to a more correct
notion about the causes of these dropsies, which causes have
been supposed to be either an *increased secretion, or an
impeded absorption,* or a rupture of a lymphatic vessel, none of
which, strictly speaking, give rise to such morbid collections
of water.   For if merely an increased secretion, or an impeded

* Hewson's Works, chapter xiii, p. 196.

absorption, was the cause of an ascites or an anasarca, then the fluid let out should resemble that contained in these cavities in living animals. The same reasoning holds good against these dropsies being occasioned by the rupture of a lymphatic vessel; that is, the fluid evacuated is not similar to what is found contained in those vessels in our experiments, where the lymph jellied on exposition to the air."

Hewson, nearly a hundred years since, in his writings on the lymphatic system, suggested that dropsies were not primary diseases, but the consequences of others; and a diseased liver, spleen, or lungs, which so often accompany these dropsies, are not so properly to be considered as giving rise to them *by causing a rupture of a lymphatic vessel*, or of obstructing the course of the lymph, as *by affecting chylification and sanguification;* for when the liver, for example, is diseased, and the bile deficient in quality or quantity, the food not being properly assimilated, *may make a bad blood*, which may affect the vessels, and may let go its water into these cavities.

And again he says, " that in these kinds of dropsies there is something more than an increased secretion, or an impeded absorption; that is, there is a perversion of the secretion, or the vessels throw out a fluid different from the natural one, which may happen rather from the exhalant arteries being altered by disease so as to change the properties of the fluid (blood) passing through them, or from the mass of blood being *vitiated* or abounding *so much* with *water*."

An impediment to the free passage of the blood through the capillaries may originate in one of three ways, and every form of dropsical effusion may be referred to one or other of them. I exclude from present consideration those forms of serous

exudation, which occurring in shut cavities are the sequel or
effect of antecedent local inflammation—such as may occur in
pleurisy, pericarditis, arachnitis, peritonitis, orchitis, or in
arthritic inflammation of joints followed by effusion—in one
sense these are dropsies, but they are not comprehended in the
diseases of which dropsy is considered a significant symptom.

The three acknowledged causes of dropsical effusion are—

1st. A poor, watery, exhausted blood.

2ndly. The presence in the blood of excrementitious or
other noxious material.

3rdly. Impediments to the free passage of the blood through
one or other of the great organs—the heart, lungs, or
liver.

The dropsical effusion which frequently accompanies spanæmia, and is often seen to result from severe hæmorrhage, particularly after parturition, arises apparently from an impoverished blood ; a blood deficient in red corpuscles, but abounding
in white colourless cells, the Leuco-cytemia of recent authors.
Blood with these qualities appears to pass with difficulty
through the capillaries, principally on account of the increased
number of the colourless cells, which, larger in size than
the red corpuscles, exhibit a remarkable tenacity for adhesion
to the walls of the vessels; the immediate effect of which is
to produce such an amount of blood stasis as to cause a transudation of the serous elements of the blood, especially in those
parts of the body most remote from the influence of the feeble
stimulus which poor blood exerts upon the heart.

The inferior extremities, where the force of gravity is
greatest, testify earliest to this dropsical condition. This form
of dropsical effusion is usually so transient, disappears so
quickly under the combined influence of nutrition and steel,

THE SIGNIFICANCE OF DROPSY.

that it is not my intention to notice it further. It is to the significance of other forms of dropsy that I desire more particularly to direct attention.

It is now generally admitted that, in the so-called blood diseases, the capillary circulation becomes impeded; so that whenever the blood is charged with morbid material, or is in any way rendered unfit for the processes of nutrition or secretion, a stagnation or imperfect movement through the capillaries becomes manifest, not only by obvious deviations in the integrity of the functions of the tissue or organ, but especially by the increased frequency of the heart's action, and the laborious efforts made by that organ to force the blood through the sluggish and congested vessels.

In the sequel to scarlet-fever, from the presence in the blood, it is assumed, of uneliminated portions of the original scarlatinal poison :—in a sudden arrest of the cutaneous secretion in certain predisposed states of the body, either of which will, we know by observation, seriously interfere with the activity of the renal functions, and will cause to be retained in the blood an excess of the chief constituent of the urine, the urea, are each examples of a dropsy originating in morbid states of the blood, in either of which the serous infiltration is diffused and universal, and pervades the tissues everywhere.

The third form, or cause of dropsical accumulations permits a more mechanical explanation. It arises from an obstruction to the current of the blood through the heart, lungs, or liver. In this division the cause of dropsy may arise either primarily in the heart—as in valvular disease of the left side,—or primarily in the lungs, and secondarily in the heart— as in emphysema and chronic bronchitis—one or both producing dilatation, and inefficient action in the right heart, and a consequent retrograde effect throughout the venous system. Dropsy from either of these causes is usually recognised as cardiac, and the serous effusion first manifesting itself in the lower extremities ultimately extends, and accumulates through the whole areolar tissue.

Lastly, the liver may become the seat of obstructive disease to the portal circulation. The effect of the obstruction here, as in cardiac dropsy, is carried back till its effects are felt in the remotest capillaries of this section of the venous system, and ascites follows.

It is little beyond thirty years since our distinguished countryman, Dr. Bright, laid the foundation, by his invaluable and original observations, for a more correct knowledge of these forms of dropsy. Tracing these effusions by post-mortem investigation, he found them significant of diseases of the renal, cardiac, pulmonary, or hepatic organs; and his researches gave a fresh and well-directed impulse to the pathological pursuits of his contemporaries and followers. But while he indicated the true method by which diseases and symptoms should be investigated, the scalpel after the first discoveries and description of morbid appearances could yield but little more. Dr. Bright, however, lived to witness the application of more minute methods of research, and he appreciated highly the results which the microscope was yielding to those who followed in the path he had opened.

It is to the very general employment of the microscope in the examination of the excretions during life, as well as of the structure of the organs and tissues after death, that we must trace the greater part of the progress that is now being made in the pathology and treatment of these diseases.

THE SIGNIFICANCE OF DROPSY. 7

By this instrument the physiologist has been made ac-
quainted with the structural elements of secreting organs, and
has been able to trace to the nucleated element of the cell
the source from whence both secretions and excretions are
derived. The pathologist, guided in his path by the light and
discoveries of physiological science, and employing similar
methods of investigation, is laying the foundation for sounder
notions of the nature of diseased action than prevailed
formerly, and is, successfully I hope, leading the way to more
effective treatment, because based on principles less theoretical
and less visionary. To the physiologist, then, we must award
the distinction of having first demonstrated the nature and
functions of the cellular elements of the tissues, and among
the foremost, because the earliest of these, must be placed J.
Goodsir, whose deductions have been confirmed by all succeeding observers.

The well-known conclusions of this physiologist are,
"that all true secretions are formed or selected by a vital
action of the nucleated cell; that the secretions are first contained in the cavity of that cell ; and he adds that both growth
and secretion are identical—the same vital process under different circumstances." These observations have been amply
confirmed by other and more recent researches, and among
those who have chiefly contributed to establish these conclusions, there are many honoured English names, whose writings
may be consulted with advantage :—Mr. Bowman, Dr. Wm.
Addison, Dr. Lionel Beale, and others. But it is perhaps to
Henle and Virchow, the distinguished professors of general
pathology and therapeutics in the University of Berlin, that
we are chiefly indebted for the extension of the physiology
of cells to the interpretation of the phenomena of disease.

It is now universally admitted that the functions of secretion, equally with the process of development and growth, are performed through the agency of cells; and that the blood in the capillaries plays simply the part of carrying nutriment and supplying the necessary stimulus and support to cell growth for the purposes of secretion. If then, from the physiological and anatomical point of view, we are taught to recognise the nucleated cell as the fundamental source of the vital processes of secretion and development, so must we from the pathological stand point equally regard the nucleated cell as involved in the processes of disease.

Accordingly we find that in every direction in which microscopic research has been hitherto made, evidence has been obtained of alterations in the character of the cellular elements—oftentimes proportioned to, and characteristic of special morbid processes; and it has been successfully shown that even the excreta during life contain marked indications of particular forms of disease, so that a microscopic examination of the effete matters thrown off will often guide us to a correct estimate of the character and progress of disease.

My present object is to direct attention to the changes which take place in the cellular structure of particular organs and tissues, with a view to determine how far these alterations may be accepted as significant of the several diseases of which dropsy is a symptom.

I would first refer to the character and appearance of the healthy epithelial gland cell of the kidney.

It is placed on what the anatomists, after Mr. Bowman's description, have called the basement membrane, but this should be more properly designated the germinal membrane, for it is from the inherent formative power of this membrane that the succession of cells is derived during life. These epithelial cells of the kidney are represented as forming a single layer, as in the intestinal canal ; and not a succession of layers superimposed one upon the other, as occurs in the bronchial mucous membrane, where the inferior layers represent young cells, which, as the older ones are thrown off, become fully developed and take their places

The individual epithelial cell of the renal tubule is polygonal in shape, and contains a nucleolus within the nucleus. The cell wall is well defined, and the contents of the cell in a healthy state appear faintly opalescent, neither opaque nor cloudy. In the early stage of renal disturbance accompanied by albuminous urine and dropsy, the epithelial gland structure of the renal tubes exhibits the simplest and earliest departure from the healthy or physiological type. It has apparently become somewhat larger, the nucleus is with difficulty seen, and the contents of the cell appear cloudy and granular. Here is the earliest manifestation of alteration of structure in the cell; and this alteration is accompanied by manifest embarrassment to the renal function. This altera-tion in the character of the renal gland cell is in the great majority of cases preceded by evidence of grave disturbance in the equilibrium of the circulation within the organ, and proofs of blood escaping in greater or smaller quantity from the Malpighian tufts are, in the acute form of renal dropsy, I believe invariable; sometimes hæmaturia is visible and palpable to the unaided eye. In other cases it requires the microscope to reveal the presence of scattered blood discs.

Within a very short period after the stage of congestion of the organ has appeared, the epithelial cells are thrown off, sometimes as isolated cells, or aggregated in twos or threes, but in most instances united together in a tubular form, constituting the epithelial casts, so familiar to the eye of the pathological microscopist. But these cells are all imperfect. This throwing off of the epithelial gland cell oftentimes in great abundance, constituting what Dr. George Johnson has characterised as a desquamative process, and has proposed to name this form of renal disorder desquamative nephritis, arises no doubt from the cell having undergone changes incompatible with its functions as a healthy secreting cell, and it therefore is cast off as effete and useless. This degradation of the cell from the physiological type we must conceive to arise from the nutritive process regulating the development of the succeeding cells from the germinal membrane (the basement membrane of Mr. Bowman) becoming embarrassed by the blood stasis. Cell after cell, so long as the embarrassment lasts, is defective and imperfect; they rapidly break up, or are thrown off entire, and to the attentive eye will afford indices of the favorable or unfavorable progress of the disease.

It cannot be too strongly impressed as a pathological fact of importance, that healthy epithelial cells of the renal tubes or of the bronchial mucous membrane, are never cast off. It is only when from defective development, being useless for the purpose of the tissue or organ in which they are formed, that they are shed, and appear among the products of excretion.

The urine becomes scanty, is loaded with albumen, and is deficient in urea, although the uric acid and the urates, are often abundant.

Here, then, is clear evidence of an alteration in the quality of the urine, coexistent with alteration in the character of the renal epithelial cell. Corresponding with, but often not noticed till a few hours after, chiefly after the first sleep, a diffused and dropsical state of the whole body shows itself. In mild cases, expressed by puffiness of the upper and lower eyelids, a slight œdema of the ankles, and back of the hands. In severe cases a diffuse œdema involving eyes and cheeks, upper and lower extremities, abdominal, and even pulmonary cavities.

In the more acute cases the pulmonary œdema gives rise to most distressing symptoms of dyspnœa. The bronchial mucous membrane becomes turgid and swollen; and cells of almost every variety belonging to this tissue are excreted in the sputa.

The rapid diffusion of the dropsy through all the textures of the body would seem to arise from the well-known physical property of imbibition.

This property of imbibition, or of swelling up on the addition of water, is possessed by all cells.

It is most apparent, the greater the difference between the specific gravity of the contents of the cell and the surrounding or external media. In the field of the microscope cells may be seen to swell up and burst when floated in distilled water. In like manner, when the tissues are soaked with the serous and watery elements of the blood, the cells not only of the areolar connective tissue swell up, enlarge, and even burst—as in extensive anasarca of the lower extremities; but, similarly, the cells of internal organs are affected, they also swell up to the manifest interruption and disturbance of the functions pertaining to them.

Concurrent with this development of a wide-spread dropsy

diffusing itself through all the tissues, it is not surprising
that the blood should, from the first, offer characters widely
deviating from the healthy standard; presenting alterations in its constituent parts, of which the most notable
are the increase in the water, the decrease of the red corpuscles, and the increase of the colourless cells, to which
must be added an increased amount of some excrementitious
products, the chief of which is urea. This form of dropsy
was once called and treated as inflammatory dropsy; and the
irritable heart, with the frequent pulse, the increased temperature of the skin, the febrile disturbance, the loss of appe-
tite, and general derangement of the functions, are symptoms of inflammatory action which justified the opinion in
those days that the disorder was essentially inflammatory.
At a period when the doctrines of inflammation played so
important a part in the theory of medicine, and when the
principles of treatment necessarily followed the theory, it was
but reasonable that the meaning of the symptoms should
be interpreted as requiring the usual measures of the anti-
phlogistic regimen.

The suddenness of the attack, usually after exposure to
wet or cold, the scanty blood-stained urine, the presence of
febrile rigors, the hurried breathing, and frequent pulse, the
hot skin, thirst and inappetency, and the general prostration,
are unequivocal signs of acute disease, having all the character of inflammatory action. The congested state of the
kidneys, the embarrassment of their function, the all but
suppressed urinary excretion, are accompanied, in the more
acute forms of the disease, by a remarkable change in the
anatomical character of these organs. A tumultuous pathological process occurs, the result of which is a great increase

in the size of the organ from a rapid accumulation of a granular matter—which appears both interstitial and intertubular—and which, when microscopically examined, seems
to be derived from an immense development of abortive
or imperfect cells, filled with the fine granular material
which appears to constitute the bulk of the organ. (Plate I,
fig. 1.) These acute cases will often run their course with
a fatality which no method of treatment appears able to
arrest.

But rapid and fatal as these cases are, they leave behind
them abundant proof that though the focus of the disease
has apparently been concentrated in the kidneys, yet that
other textures have been similarly affected, and that cell
development in other organs is equally the seat of deterioration and decay.

It is, however, chiefly by the study of cases which run a
more sluggish course, either passing from an acute form to
the chronic, or originating more slowly, with less evidence of
a so-called inflammatory origin, that the wide-spread degeneration of cell growth can be more clearly and satisfactorily
demonstrated. As the renal disturbance assumes a more
chronic and manageable form, there takes place a marked
alteration in the character of the effete cells which are washed
out of the tubules, and which appear in the urine.

The epithelial cell is now less characteristic of the standard
cell. Its nucleus is no longer visible. The cells are filled
with highly resplendent granules, and we now observe, in
greater abundance, these granule cells, which were once
called Gluge's inflammatory corpuscles. This has led many
to think that the presence of these granule cells is a proof of
inflammatory action.

But these granule cells are abortive epithelial cells; they are present, I shall presently show, in all disordered conditions of mucous membranes, they rapidly break up and are dispersed, and the remains of them in the form of isolated highly resplendent granules, or grouped together in twos or threes, sometimes in greater number, presenting grape-like clusters of granules (mulberry) without any cell-wall, are constant objects in the field of the microscope.

Virchow says of these granule cells *or* inflammatory corpuscle, "A cell never remains, for any length of time, in the state of a granule cell; but as soon as it has entered into this stage, the nucleus generally disappears at once, and ultimately the membrane also; probably by a species of solution. Then we have the simple granule globule, or, as it was formerly called, inflammatory globule (exudation corpuscle), which Gluge first described under this name. Gluge here made a mistake, common to early stages of microscopy. He saw, when examining a kidney, bodies of this sort in the interior of a canal, which he took for a blood-vessel. This happening at a time when the doctrine of blood stasis was most in vogue, he imagined he had before him a vessel with stagnating contents, and which were disintegrating and generating inflammatory globules. Unfortunately the blood-vessel was a uriniferous tubule; what he termed inflammatory globules are degenerated renal epithelium." *

The body we call a granule globule, is now to be regarded as the first distinct proof of degeneration, when the cell no longer retains its existence as a cell; for membrane and nucleus have completely passed away. These alterations of cell structure may be traced in other mucous membranes

* 'Cellular Pathology,' p. 338.

besides the kidneys. But the mucous membranes are not
alone in furnishing evidence of a wide spread disorder.
I have already casually alluded to the defect in the composition of the blood, the increase of water and decrease
of the blood corpuscles. When we recollect that this fluid
bathes the germinal membranes on which the epithelial cells
are developed, and brings to the germs of these cells the
necessary stimulus for their growth, we can hardly be sur-
prised in the face of abortive cells from the epithelial textures
generally, to find that the fluid which furnishes the material
for their growth should be defective and poor. Not only are
the blood corpuscles as estimated by weight deficient, but
the fluid in which they live and move, the liquor sanguinis, has
become altered in quality, and of lower specific gravity than
in healthy blood. The effect of this is immediate on the contents of the blood corpuscle ; for there must be a relative equa-
lity between the density of the contents of the blood corpuscle
and the fluid in which it floats, or the process of exosmosis
would rapidly restore the equilibrium. The great extent to
which the diminution of the number of blood corpuscles takes
place in renal dropsy is in a great measure dependent on this
cause ; as the hydræmic or watery serum causes the breaking
up and destruction of the blood corpuscle, while other causes
prevent their renewal in any degree proportioned to their
loss.

The nutritive functions have long been disturbed ; the
blood has become impoverished, and all that depends on it
for the stimulus of healthy development suffers. My esteemed
and distinguished friend, Mr. Henry Power, has suggested
that the presence of urea in the blood in excess may
and probably does interfere with the development of new

blood corpuscles, as well as spoil or poison those already
formed.

It has been physiologically shown that the functions of
secretion are carried on by the agency of cells. I think
it must be apparent that the effusion of a dropsical fluid into
the chief tissues of the blood, such as occurs in renal dropsy,
can hardly be dependent on the degeneration of only one
class of gland-cell, however important the function of those
cells may be. I think, therefore, it will not be an unex-
pected result, to find that the imperfect development and
abortive character of the renal cell, originating as that imperfection does, not from any local cause of irritation, but
from general constitutional causes, of which a poor and
watery blood is one of the most manifest, is likely to be
accompanied by an imperfection of cell development in other
organs and structures, although, perhaps, neither to the extent
nor with such hazardous consequences as in the kidneys.

The glandular epithelial cells of these organs are those
which first give notice of the alteration both of function and
structure.

The very presence of albumen in the urine is assurance of
the imperfection of these cells. But this deterioration of cell
growth is not confined, as was at first thought, to that organ
whose embarrassment of function is earliest recognised.

Even in the acute form of Morbus Brightii cases which have
run their fatal course in a few weeks the epithelial cells of
other parts present a granular and imperfect appearance. The
epithelium of the mouth, throat, and alimentary passages is
granular, and sometimes even fatty, the pavement epithelium
of the bladder often most prominently so. The epithelial
cells of the bronchial mucous membrane are cloudy and gra-

nular, and accompanied by evidence of cellular deterioration identical in character to what we witness in the renal tubes.

Even in the most acute cases structural changes in the heart-fibre are present.

The small arteries which lead to the epithelial layers are everywhere diseased; and not only in the most advanced forms of renal degeneration, such as that known as the amyloid degeneration, but in the other various forms of renal dropsy, the small arteries of the whole digestive tract, from the buccal cavity to the anus, are similarly affected.*

The inevitable result of this wide-spread decay is that the parts and cells which are the seat of it become totally unfit and incapable of ministering to the functions either of nutrition or excretion. The gland-cells can no longer perform the function of secretion, and the vessels can no longer supply nutrition to the tissues from which the epithelial gland-cell is formed.

I propose to offer a few proofs of this wide-spread degeneration.

The bronchial mucous membrane exhibits remarkable proofs of the wide-spread degeneration of tissue. Plate I, fig. 4, represents a vertical section through one of the smaller bronchial tubes. No trace of ciliated epithelium is visible; the successive layers of cells, as they form, are more indicative of the mucous corpuscle or effete cell than of the layers seen in healthy tissue. Immediately beneath the basement membrane the fibro-elastic tissue is seen studded with fat-granules, and subordinate to it the layer of unstriped muscle is seen also fatty and degenerating. Figs. 5 and 6 represent these layers separately and more highly magnified.

* Virchow, p. 378.

2

The expectoration in these cases of morbus Brightii is represented in fig. 3, and presents the usual evidence of imperfect cell development invariably present when a mucous membrane is the seat of nutritive or irritative disturbance.

Nor must the change which takes place in the ordinary fat-cell of the subcutaneous connective tissue be overlooked ; this, which in health contains fat more or less solid, and which may be considered to represent its ordinary nutritive contents, in these states of general anasarca contains only a few fluid drops of oily-looking fat, but is crammed to over-distension with a thin, serous, albuminous fluid.

With these facts before us, we must be led to the conviction that the agency of deterioration in renal dropsy is not a local agent, manifesting itself only in renal cells, but that it is some wide-spread depressing influence, pervading the organism ; operating, perhaps, less palpably, but not less fatally, everywhere.

I may here be permitted to remark, with regard to this universal decadence, that, throughout the entire series of epithelial mucous membranes, there appears to exist a uniform law of decadence common to all the epithelial cells, whatever the function of those cells may be. So that whether they be the scaly or pavement, the spheroidal or glandular, the oval or ciliated—whether the function of the cell be secretory or simply protective—when under the influence of a morbid cause, they severally exhibit a departure from the healthy type of the tissue to which they belong in a direction common to them all.

They first become cloudy, swell, and look rounded, and apparently filled with a fine granular matter, in which the nucleus is concealed ; this is the so-called mucous cor-

muscle; the nucleus, in many of these cells, becomes much
larger in appearance, and the contents more distinctly granular. All these cells may rapidly disintegrate, and yield,
by their breaking up, the mucin which is so abundant in all
catarrhal affections in which these cells are so numerous.
Next in order we meet with cells with highly resplendent
nuclei, refracting light highly. These fatty nuclei accompany cells of much larger diameter. These are the so-called
Gluge's inflammatory corpuscles. Other cells continue to
exhibit well-formed nuclei, but differing materially in form
from those already noticed. They are smaller in diameter
than the fat-granule-cell (Gluge's). The nucleus may be
made very distinct by dilute acetic acid; and it presents
various forms or appearances—reniform, trefoiled, as if un-
dergoing multiplication by division. The true pus-cell presents the conditions of the latter, exhibiting a more or less
distinctly trefoiled or reniform nucleus. These several
forms of cell, in the case of those epithelial textures which
are composed of numerous layers of cells, as the bronchial
mucous membrane, may be seen almost simultaneously, or
at any rate in very rapid succession.

Whenever a disturbing cause, irritative or inflammatory, exercises its influence on epithelial membrane, these
appear to be the successive modifications which the cells
undergo.

There is, however, one circumstance connected with these
modifications of the cellular elements of mucous membranes
which must be kept in view. It is the relative frequency or
infrequency of the pus-cell from these epithelial structures.
It is very common from some, equally rare from others. It
is very common from the whole length of the pulmonary

mucous membrane, from the pelvis of the kidney, from the ureters, bladder, or urethra. It is equally rare from the gastrointestinal track, or from the tubuli uriniferi.

The explanation of this fact is found in the arrangement of the cellular elements in these several varieties of epithelial structure.

In the first-named parts the cells are superimposed in a succession of layers. (Plate I, fig. 4.) Any disturbing cause leading to the shedding of the first series, and continuing its irritating influence, prevents the cells beneath either from arriving at maturity, or so modifies their development that a succession of transitional cells follows; and where the irritation assumes the form of the so-called inflammatory action, the pus-cell is produced in great abundance.

The formation of these cells, it may be observed, is not at the expense of the integrity of the tissue out of which they are formed.

On the other hand, in the gastro-intestinal and renal layers the epithelial cells occupy but a single row, and are developed directly from the germinal or basement membrane. Hence, although they undergo transitional states, passing from the true cell to the granular and mucous cell, they rarely possess the character of the pus-cell, and when they do so can only become developed at the expense of the subjacent tissue, or, in other words, can only be formed by an ulcerative process, with loss of substance.

To return to the subject of the condition of the cells in other organs in Bright's disease.

If we now turn to the inner parts of the body, when a post-mortem examination permits us to investigate the state of parts hidden from us during life, in all those cases in which fluid has been present in the abdominal cavity, the abdominal serous membrane presents an opaque aspect, different from what we witness in cases, for instance, of violent death, where this membrane looks translucent and clear, smooth and shining.

If a portion of the peritoneum be scraped, the wavy fibrous structure and the tesselated epithelial cells have always appeared to me highly granular, participating in the general cloudy character of the epithelial cells elsewhere.

But the surface of the heart—the exocardium—particularly in the majority of cases of morbus Brightii, exhibits those well-known spots called the *maculæ albidæ*, shining, opalescent and opaque patches, of which pathologists have noticed two varieties—one variety looking like a morsel of false membrane laid on and adhering to the subjacent serous surface, with a well-defined margin, which can be raised and peeled off. These appear to be in the nature of inflammatory products, although the history of the case rarely yields any evidence of any antecedent pericardial attacks. This form is, however, infrequent as compared with the next, in which the opacity gradually merges into the surrounding tissue. There is no appearance of a raised edge, and the patch looks simply like a milky white stain.

The tesselated epithelium of this surface is lost, and in its place nothing but a débris of granular matter can be seen, interspersed with coarse interlacing fibres, which seem to inclose the granules, together with numerous fat-granules. (Plate II, fig. 1.) The muscular walls of the heart are not usually unhealthy looking to the eye, or flabby in texture. These conditions would prove nothing; but if a careful microscopic examination of the muscular substance be made,

proof may be obtained that here also is degeneration and
decay. There is a universal tendency to fatty and granular
degeneration.

The muscular striæ, instead of being clear and distinct
and well-defined, are studded with granules, which here and
there, in the larger form, become resplendent and highly
refractive, presenting all the character of a fatty débris,
which they really are, as may be clearly proved by the
action of ether, which quickly removes them, leaving the
fibrillæ naked and destitute in these spots, of all indications
of striæ. (Plate II, fig. 2.)

Not only is the evidence of degeneration to be observed in
the muscular structure of the heart—both in ventricles and
auricles—but oftentimes opaque spots are seen studding the
commencement of the aorta, and extending in patches, to a
greater or less extent, throughout the vascular system.

Figs. 3 and 4, Plate II, represent the microscopic appearances
of one of these so-called atheromatous patches. It reveals
the presence of much fatty débris, with here and there a
plate or two of cholesterine. Fig. 4 represents a vertical
section through one of these aortic patches. Both were
taken from chronic cases of morbus Brightii.

The liver, in the majority of fatal cases of morbus Brightii,
affords unequivocal proof of the disturbance which this organ
suffers. Every cell appears loaded with fat. No pigment-
grains are present, but the liver-cells appear overcharged
with large, round, resplendent fat-granules, giving such a
fatty character to this organ that bacony liver is the term
often applied to it. The ordinary appearance of the liver-
cell in morbus Brightii is represented in fig. 5, Plate II.

If one of the minute nodules from the surface of a kidney

in almost any form of morbus Brightii except the acute form, be separated and examined with the microscope, the convoluted tubes appear filled with detached cells, surrounded by a fine granular matter, with here and there fatty débris scattered among them. (Fig. 6, Plate II.)

May we not now appreciate the significance of that form of dropsy which, associated with albuminous urine as one of its earliest and most easily recognised conditions, pervades all the tissues, infiltrates every cell, interferes with and stagnates every function, and oftentimes becomes the immediate cause of death, by literally drowning the individual in his own fluids.

But, furthermore, this form of dropsy signifies a wide-spread deterioration of cell development; it signifies, not a local disease of the kidneys, but a decay and depreciation of tissue everywhere. For if we obtain evidence of deviations from so many remote points, we may safely infer that a like decay or deterioration of structure exists elsewhere.

Now, these reflections would be regarded but as a barren speculation, or at most a few favourite pathological facts, if they rested here.

I propose, before the close of these lectures, to submit for your consideration certain principles which I believe should govern the treatment of all cases of renal dropsy. Principles not at variance with those practised by all our most enlightened physicians; although, perhaps, they may now be advocated and based on facts not hitherto universally adopted.

Before, however, I refer to this branch of my subject, I am very desirous of making some observations on two points connected with the subject of renal degeneration, with a view of clearing up, if possible, a certain obscurity which still hangs over them.

The first is, an inquiry into the nature and origin of the tube-casts in morbus Brightii.

The second is, the source and channel whence the albumen is derived in the same form of disease.

Of the nature and origin of the casts of the tubes in renal dropsy, great diversity of opinion still prevails.

The most recently expressed opinions on this subject still leave the question unsettled and undetermined.

Dr. Beale, in his excellent and recent work on the urine and urinous deposits,* in his account of these uriniferous casts, says, " Great difference of opinion has been expressed with reference to the nature of the material of which the cast is composed. By some it is termed fibrine; but the striated appearance always present in coagula of this substance is not found in the cast. Others have considered the cast was composed of albumen ; but it is not rendered opaque by means of those reagents which produce precipitates in albuminous solutions. Not more than five years since it was stated by two observers in France and Germany, of high reputation, that the cast really consisted of the basement membrane of the uriniferous tube;" and Dr. Beale very properly remarks, " How such a statement could be made by any one possessing even a slight knowledge of the anatomy of tissues it is difficult to conceive."

Dr. Beale then goes on to say, " The transparent material probably consists of a peculiar modification of an albuminous matter, possessing somewhat the same character as the walls of some epithelial cells. I think it not improbable that these casts of the uriniferous tubes may really be composed of the materials which in health form the substance of epithelial

* Second Edition, 1861.

cells. In disease this substance, perhaps somewhat altered, or not perfectly formed, collects in the uriniferous tubes, and coagulates there. This receives some support from the fact that, occasionally, casts are formed although no albumen passes into the urine. According to this notion, it is possible that a cast might be formed quite independently of any congestion or morbid condition of the Malpighian tufts; but, as a general rule, there can be no doubt that serum escapes, and albumen is found in the urine."—P. 60.

Thus far Dr. Beale.

LECTURE II.

MR. PRESIDENT AND GENTLEMEN,—The purport of my last lecture was to show how wide-spread is the evidence of degeneration and texture in Renal dropsy; and that the dropsy and albuminous urine are significant, not simply of renal derangement, but of a general decadence of the cellular elements of various and distant tissues.

The inference I would deduce from these facts is that in the treatment of these disorders our efforts should be directed, not chiefly to the functions of the kidneys, but mainly to the renovation of the blood, and the support and maintenance of its cell-forming power.

Before I more directly address myself to a few remarks on the subject of treatment, there are two points of some interest in renal pathology, to which I adverted at the close of the last lecture, to which I am desirous of asking your attention. These are—

1. An inquiry into the nature and origin of the urinary tube-casts in morbus Brightii.

2. The source and channel whence the albumen is derived in the same form of disease.

I have already referred to the fact of the great diversity of opinion which prevails as to the nature of these casts, and I quoted from Dr. Lionel Beale's last edition of his work on the urine and urinary deposits, his remarks on this subject, which still leave the question unsettled.

The two subjects—the nature and the origin of the tube-casts, and the source whence the albumen is derived,—are, I believe, intimately connected together; in fact, may be said to be mutually dependent.

The point I propose to consider is whether much of the albumen in morbus Brightii is not, probably, derived from the breaking up and disintegration of the abortive and futile cells, which are formed in these cases with a rapidity which is so characteristic of all defective cells, it being also a leading feature of all such cellular formations that, being deficient in the most essential element of their development —the nucleus—their duration is but transitory, and they rapidly break up, perish, and disappear.*

It is some years since I ventured to express an opinion that the so-called waxy or hyaline casts were strictly ana-logous to what is found formed by other epithelial surfaces having the character of mucous membranes.†

Further investigation into this subject has convinced me that in their nature they differ but little, except in their tubular form or appearance, from what is thrown off from the bronchial mucous membrane under the influence of irritation or the so-called inflammatory causes. I have traced these excretory matters in all the commoner forms of pulmonary disorder; and I have traced from the ordinary sputa of simple catarrh, through the various grades of bronchitis—especially in that somewhat unusual form, the tubular or

* Virchow, p. 11.
† 'On Dropsy,' 2nd edition, p. 136.

plastic bronchitis, as well as capillary bronchitis—in pneumonia, both in the mild and severe forms, even in phthisis,
types of nearly all the forms of casts found in renal dropsy.

Plates III and IV represent these various forms of sputa.
In fig. 1 is portrayed the hyaline appearance of the sputa,
containing a few large spherical cells (mucous corpuscles), with
one large granule-cell—often called a pigment-cell, from
its being in many cases deeply coloured greyish or black,
particularly in the sputa of those living in large towns.

These sputa are the type of the hyaline casts seen in atro-
phying kidneys, in the gouty kidney, and in the last and
more favorable stage of the curable cases of renal dropsy.
In these latter cases, as I have elsewhere remarked, it signifies a simple catarrhal state of the renal tubes. That is
a state in which but few abortive or imperfect cells are
formed, and consequently but few cast off. In all forms of
gouty kidney these hyaline casts are present, and they signify
a like catarrhal condition of the renal tubes. It must be
recollected that their presence by no means signifies an
atrophy or shrinking of the kidneys, although they are commonly present in most instances of gouty kidney. The
atrophic process depends on conditions altogether different
from those present in morbus Brightii. The present occasion does not permit me to do more than allude to this state
of the gouty kidney.

The representation of the sputa in ordinary bronchitis does
not differ from those which are seen in the bronchitis of those
suffering from renal dropsy. In these sputa we find all the
cell-elements found in the sediment of the severer forms of
albuminuria. Plate I, fig. 3, affords a proof that the bronchial
mucous membrane gives cell products differing only in the

absence of a tubular arrangement or grouping, but identical
in other respects with what can be seen in any chronic case
of morbus Brightii other than in the stage of congestion.
But the sputa in plastic and capillary bronchitis often present
appearances more strictly typical of the casts of the renal
tubes. These are very analogous to the fibrinous casts of
second stage of acute morbus Brightii (Plate III, fig. 2),
and the type of the granular epithelial cast is more distinctly obvious in the sputa of capillary bronchitis. (Plate
III, fig. 3.)

The sputa in pneumonia possess many features in common
with the casts of the inflammatory or acute stage of morbus
Brightii.

The blood-casts, or as they are sometimes called fibrinous
blood-casts, always present in the early stage of the dropsy
after scarlet fever, have their analogy in the rust-coloured or
more deeply stained sputa of pneumonia.

Plate IV represents the sputa in various stages and degrees
of severity in pneumonia.

Figs. 4 and 5 are representations of the rust-coloured
and blood-stained sputa in severe cases. The cellular elements present are identical with those seen in the casts
in the urine in the stage of hæmaturia after scarlet
fever, and the stage of engorgement of the kidneys in the
early stage of acute morbus Brightii. In the milder forms
of pneumonia, where the expectoration is but slightly
tinged (figs. 1, 2, 3), scarcely deeper than a Sienna orange
colour, blood-discs are not frequently visible; but large cells,
similar to the so-called pigment-cells of ordinary bronchial
catarrh, and which give to the sputa that steel-gray colour
so familiar to all, appear to be the cells which have most

affinity for the colouring matter derived from the hæmatin;
for these cells, in the mild forms of pulmonary inflammation, are alone coloured. It will be seen that the deeper
colour, in the rust-coloured and blood-coloured sputa, is due
to the increased number of blood-corpuscles, and the propor-
tional increase in the hæmatin tinging all the cells except
those derived from the mouth and cheeks. Three cells of
squamous epithelium in the corner of the figures remain
uncoloured.

Fig. 6 is the expectoration of the stage of liquefaction of
the croupous product, and consists of an abundance of mucus-
and pus-cells. These forms find their analogue in those
casts of the renal tubes which appear in the sequel to the
acute stage of cases of morbus Brightii, which present the
indications of becoming curable. This form of sediment is
represented in my work on Dropsy (Plate VIII, figs. 13, 14,
15), and portray cells similar in all respects to those which
the terminal period of pneumonia exhibits.

Lastly, in phthisis the expectoration displays all the
characteristic cell and fatty aggregations which appear in
the urinary sediment in cases of extreme fatty or amyloid
degeneration of the kidneys, forms of renal disease often
associated with phthisis and cancer. If the figures representing the urinary deposit in a case of phthisis (Plate VII,
figs. 1, 2, 3) in the above work, as well as the figs. 1 and
2, Plate VIII, of the same be compared with the fig. 4,
Plate III, of the present lectures, the identity of the cellular
elements will become conclusively apparent.

I think, then, it cannot be denied by those who are familiar
with the microscopic appearances of the sputa in the different
forms of pulmonary disorder, that varieties of abortive, dete-

riorated, and depraved epithelial cell growth present in these excreta are identical in appearance with those which are seen in the renal casts, the only distinction being in the apparently tubular form of the one, and the more diffluent aspect of the other. Yet I have occasionally, and after some patient research, found, especially in chronic phthisis, and once in capillary bronchitis, casts in all respects, except in size, identical with renal casts. In pulmonary diseases these excretory matters are derived from the metamorphosis of the epithelial elements of the bronchial mucous membrane. Can we hesitate to adopt the proposition that strictly analogous appearances occurring in the renal tubes are also derived from the metamorphosis of the abortive epithelial elements of the renal tubes? If this view be accepted, there is no longer any difficulty in understanding the nature and source of the renal casts. Proportioned to the intensity and character of the disturbing or irritating cause, we observe either—

I. Fibrinous blood-casts corresponding to what is seen in pneumonia.

II. Epithelial granular casts corresponding to what is seen in bronchitis.

III. Epithelial and purulent and granular casts, corresponding to the cellular elements in acute bronchitis and the stage of resolution in pneumonia; hyaline or transparent casts, as in simple catarrh; fatty casts, as is seen in phthisis.

The fibrinous blood-casts are clearly derived from a hæmorrhage into renal tubes, and they evidently consist of blood-globules and fibrinous matter coagulated in the tubes; and the rust-coloured sputa of pneumonia is similarly formed.

The granular epithelial casts consist of epithelial cells, more granular than the healthy glandular epithelial cell; in fact, the cell in the earliest state of depraved metamorphosis. Many of these abortive cells break up and disintegrate, perhaps as soon as formed, and their granular or mucin-like contents, entangling therein cells which are swept away by the fluids from behind, present to the eye the appearance of epithelial cells held together by a fine granular material. The same conditions are apparent in the viscid sputa of bronchitis, and especially in bronchial catarrh.

The pus-cast is identical with what is seen in pneumonia and in capillary bronchitis. The epithelial cell, instead of being simply abortive, cloudy, and granular, has degenerated into the more rapidly growing pus-cell. This is also washed away by the current from behind, and so long as the pus or mucus is derived from the epithelial elements only of the renal tube it preserves this tubular appearance. But if, as in cases of scrofulous or calculous pyelitis, the pus is derived from the cellular elements of the interstitial tissue, then the pus is no longer held together in tubular-formed casts, but becomes freely diffused through the urine as fluid pus, a condition analogous to what is seen in tubercular ulceration of the lungs. The fatty casts represent the most advanced state of degeneration. The cells contain large aggregations of fatty nuclei. Sometimes the cells are large compound cells, with numerous highly resplendent nuclei; accompanying these are fatty granules, varying in size, sometimes aggregated together, sometimes free.

These appearances are familiar to us as occurring most frequently in cases of phthisis, where there is albuminous urine, and where the kidneys are eventually found with the cha-

racters of the waxy or spermaceti-like (lardaceous or amyloid)
degeneration.

The hyaline or transparent cast, so identical in appearance
with what comes from mucous membranes under the simple
form of irritation, as in ordinary bronchial catarrh, represents
I believe the terminal period of the equally milder forms of
renal disturbance, as well as the more severe ones of atrophy.
In all those curable cases of albuminuria which follow scarlet
fever, so soon as the renal engorgement with its fibrinous
blood-casts has given place to the epithelial granular casts,
they in their turn, slowly and *pari passu*, with the diminution, and even disappearance of the albumen from the urine,
are followed by these hyaline or transparent casts, and
represent, I think, a state of the tubes analogous to ordinary
catarrh, that is, mucous-cells (uninuclear) are formed, which
quickly disintegrate and break up; and this disintegration
produces the colourless mucin-like material, transparent and
glassy, with here and there a resplendent granule, the abortive
nucleus of one of these defective cells. (Plate III, fig. 1.)

The hyaline-casts, even the most delicate and transparent,
always contain, or are accompanied by resplendent nuclei;
the nuclei doubtless of the disintegrated cells.

These hyaline-casts are very frequent in cases of gouty
kidney, especially where the amount of albumen is not large.
In the more serious forms of albuminuria their presence always
marks a period of comparative improvement and diminution of the dropsy; and a return to the formation of cells
more adapted to perform the function of excreting the usual
urinary constituents.

Again, as a general rule, those cases eventually do best
in which either the so-called pus cells, or even pus-casts,

3

that is, cells with a trefoiled or reniform nucleus, are mixed
up with, or take the place of the epithelial casts; for these
pus-cells, or mucous-cells, really represent a safer direction for cell development to take than the highly fatty, or
highly granular, or the compound granule-cells, which are the
types of the more intractable forms of renal degeneration.

I have, therefore, no hesitation in expressing my conviction that these casts are derived from the metamorphosis or
breaking up of the epithelial cells of the renal tubes, ex-
cepting in the case of the fibrinous blood-cast, which appears
to be formed by the coagulation of the fibrine entangling
blood-corpuscles within it, and is therefore formed directly
by hæmorrhage. In all other forms of the so-called tube
casts, they are derived from the metamorphosis of cells in
various stages of degeneration and decay; for it must be
recollected that all these casts contain evidence of broken up
cell structure.

I now approach the second branch of these observations,—
the evidence which suggests that the albumen in albuminous
urine is derived as a secretion from the abortive cloudy granular cells which fill the uriniferous tubes of all kidneys
yielding albuminous urine.

Whence is the albumen derived which appears in the urine
so abundantly in cases of albuminuria?

It is generally believed to drain through the Malpighian
capillaries. It is affirmed that the serous elements of the
blood percolate through these capillaries, which, in health,
are supposed to furnish only the aqueous constituent of the
urine. But if this were so, then the urine should contain
not albumen alone, but the usual proportion of salts which
make up the constituents of the serum of the blood. But

this is impossible to prove, because the saline constituents of the urine of health do not materially differ, except in quantity, both relative and absolute, from those which are present in the serum of the blood.

Carbonates, sulphates, phosphates, chlorides of sodium and potassium, lime, and magnesia, in varying proportions, are present in both fluids. Some salts are found in the urine which are not present in the serum of the blood ; but there are no salts in the serum which are not present in healthy urine. The chemical analysis of the urine, then, throws no light on the source from whence the albumen comes, and we still are left to conjecture, or to further investigation, to trace the channel through which so large a quantity of albumen is carried out of the system.

The explanation hitherto offered, that it is a simple percolation of the serous elements of the blood through the Malpighian capillaries, occasioned by obstructed circulation, has always appeared to me unsatisfactory.

1st. It is too mechanical.

2ndly. So direct a drain would, it might be supposed, have a corresponding influence in lessening the watery or serous character of the blood in Bright's disease. Yet the opposite is notorious : for the greater the albuminous drain through the kidneys the more watery and serous does the blood become.

M. Robin has proposed a theory to explain the presence of albumen of the urine.

He considers that in health, albumen, as an excrementitious product, is decomposed in the blood by the functions of respiration ; and that the nitrogenous residue of this combustion, urea and uric acid, are eliminated by the urine. Whatever, therefore, interferes with this metamorphosis of the

albumen in the lungs causes its presence in the renal secretion. Thus, albumen is present in many pulmonary disorders—capillary bronchitis, phthisis, pneumonia, and certain
cardiac affections.

M. Robin concludes that, when the respiratory process of
combustion is too feeble to destroy the whole of the albumen
which should be consumed in a given time, the general
vitality is diminished; and thus, more or less albumen is
allowed to pass into the urine: in fact, just so much as
escapes transformation into urea and uric acid. The theory
is ingenious and plausible; but it will not stand the test of
clinical proof. The urine is albuminous in some cases of
capillary bronchitis, in some cases of pneumonia, phthisis,
and cardiac disease; even in some cases of emphysema and
chronic bronchitis, but not in all. The hypothesis must fall,
if (the assumed conditions being present) the proof fails
even in one instance.

There are various physiological experiments and observations which, undeniably, favour the hitherto received opinion
that the albumen of the urine is obtained directly from the
blood. Bernard has shown that crude albumen injected into
the jugular vein produces temporary albuminuria. And he
further remarks that, in health, if the albumen of two or
three raw eggs be swallowed, albumen will appear in the
urine. I have tried, but have not been able to verify this
experiment.

The liver is supposed to possess a powerful modifying
agency on albuminous matters. Lehmann declares that 30
per cent. of albumen entering the liver by the portal vein,
disappears in its passage through that organ, and cannot be
found in the hepatic vein.

Dr. Parkes is inclined to the opinion that the liver plays an important part in the development of albuminuria; he thinks, through some failure in preparation, either by the stomach or the liver, albumen enters the right side of the heart, still in a crude state, and in a condition similar to that introduced into the jugular vein in Bernard's experiment.

And he very pertinently adds, " many cases," I am inclined to say all, " appear to be of blood origin, and among the many common antecedents of Bright's disease are circumstances of diet and mode of life impairing the processes of the stomach and liver. In how many cases," he asks, " although no liver disease was suspected during life, do we find the structure of this organ seriously diseased. In the history of Bright's disease there are many reasons for believing that the nutrition of the tissues is early and deeply affected."

Even admitting the soundness of this view, it still offers as an explanation but a simple mechanical filtration of the serous elements of the blood, the albuminous matters, through the walls of the capillaries arising from blood stasis. The sluggish current delayed in the capillaries, parts with its albuminous constituents, which infiltrate the surrounding tissue. In this way it is supposed that the renal circulation being impeded and overcharged with highly albuminized blood the excess of albuminous material may find its way into the renal tubes, and finally appear in the urine. This explanation may be sufficiently intelligible for the early stages, particularly the acute stage of morbus Brightii. But will it suffice to account for the large proportion of albumen which continues in the urine in chronic cases for months, and as the experience of many of us can testify,

for years, in cases that have lost all trace of disease, except
that which is still considered the most significant, the albumen in the urine.

It appears to me more consistent with the recent researches
of pathologists, to conceive that this abundant excretory
product is, at any rate in these chronic cases of albuminuria,
more immediately derived from the agency of cells; and if
so, we must consider the albumen in the urine in the light of
a secretion. Then, if as a secretion, whence derived? My
answer is either from the abortive casts, or from the disintegration and rapid breaking up of these imperfect cells, which
are in constant and rapid formation, and which are generated in the place of the true and vigorous gland-cell, whose
office it would be to secrete the constituents only of ordinary
urine.

Can any proof be adduced in favour of this opinion?
Analogy is not proof, but analogy, I think, justifies it. It is
well known that in pneumonia all the chloride of sodium
which should appear in the urine, disappears from that excretion, and makes its appearance in the sputa from the
pulmonary-cells. Can we, for a moment, suppose that this
chloride is a simple filtration of the salt from the blood
through the walls of the capillaries in the air-cells? What
determines its presence here, rather than in any other tissue,
but that the cells attract this chloride as essential to their
development? The chloride is absent from the urine, and
present in the sputa only so long as these cells are formed
and thrown off. Its absence from the urine marks the period
of hepatization, and as liquefaction of the exuded product
goes on, and the rusty sputa slowly gives way to a free, purulent, and eventually a muco-purulent expectoration, the

chloride disappears from the pulmonary exudation, and re-appears in the urine.

But what exercises this force of attraction? Not simply the condition of the inflammatory process; for if so, in-flammatory tissues generally should attract the chlorides, and in every form of inflammation they should be absent from the urine.

The sputa of pneumonic inflammation are derived from the fibro-serous coat of the air-cavity, the cells of which, while attracting and forming the fibrinous and croupons material possess apparently a special affinity for the chlorides.

It is an attraction essential, perhaps, to the development of the abortive cells which accompany the fibrinous and croupons exudation, and continues until ulterior changes in the cha-racter of the excreted matters have become perfected.

Again, in gouty inflammation, we know, from the re-searches of Dr. Garrod, that the essence of the inflammatory process is a deposit in the cartilaginous, ligamentous, tendi-nous, and osseous tissues of uric acid, and its soda base.

Here, again, there cannot be simple transudation of the urate through the walls of the capillary blood-vessels.

For cartilage is non-vascular: the blood, however, has been proved to contain uric acid in excess in gout. How, then, can it find its way to the non-vascular cartilaginous tissue, except by a special or peculiar affinity which the cartilage-cell exercises for the excrementitious matter when it accumulates, or is not freely carried off by the kidneys.

We daily recognise, and can, during life, satisfactorily demonstrate this affinity of cartilage-cells for uric acid and its soda base. The cartilages of the ear, in gouty habits, are the well-known seat of these uric acid deposits. Dr.

Garrod was, I believe, the first to point out this pathological fact, and use it as a test of distinction between true gout and rheumatism. It may at all times be applied to any individual in whom there lurks the gouty habit. Thus the morbid matter of gout, the uric acid, is not deposited, hap-hazard, here or there; but only in certain well-defined tissues, and these appear to be the cells of cartilage, ligament, tendon, and bone, which seem to be endowed with an elective or selective power; and attract to themselves this material, which remains persistently in the cells of the tissue in which it is deposited.

Again, why in acute rheumatic fever is there so marked a disposition to the accumulation of the fibrinous elements of the blood on the valves of the heart as well as on the exocardial membrane, but that the cellular elements of these tissues exercise a certain attractive force by which fibrine is drawn from the blood? The cellular elements of the serous surface, as Virchow has shown, take up this excess of fibrine; the process, therefore, is not a simple filtration or mechanical transudation of the fibrine, as was once conceived, but an example of perverted cell nutrition.

Moreover, it appears to be difficult to understand how ulterior changes could take place in the material deposited on the valves of the heart, if, as I shall hereafter endeavour to show, it was a simple filtrate of fibrine, unaccompanied by any cellular elements. How could it as pure fibrine, such as we recognise it when obtained direct from the blood by whipping, undergo either purulent, fatty, or earthy degeneration, except through the agency of cells?

Again, in regard to the phenomena of some blood-poisons, for instance, syphilis, why should certain structures be specially affected, as others are exempt from the secondary effects of this disease ? Why are the iris, the periosteal and osseous structures, the skin, and certain portions of the epithelial membranes, the chief seats of its manifestations, but that the cellular elements of those parts exercise a species of affinity or selection for certain morbific agents ? Again, why in jaundice should there be that remarkable difference between the colour of the conjunctiva and the skin, and the internal parts of the mouth; the intense orange tinge of the two former contrasting so strangely with the red natural-looking colour of the inside of the lips, cheek, and tongue ; but that the cells of the orange-stained tissues possess an elective or selective power not possessed by the epithelial cells of the alimentary canal, for the pigmentary element of the bile retained in the blood in those forms of liver disorders giving rise to jaundice. Moreover, in this disorder the renal epithelial-cell appears to possess this selective power to a great degree, hence so large a portion of the bile-pigments in jaundice finds its outlet through the kidneys.

I must therefore, venture to express my conviction that if, as we may reasonably suppose, the chlorides in pneumonia are excreted through the agency of the cellular elements thrown off in the sputa,—if the uric acid compounds in gout find their way from the blood through the agency and affinity of cartilage and other cells; if in the so-called inflammatory process of serous surfaces the fibrinous element of the blood is fixed in those tissues as an exudation chiefly through the agency of cellular affinity; if in jaundice only certain cells take up the retained bile-pigment, so I would conclude that the albuminous matter, so persistently and continuously excreted in chronic morbus Brightii (albuminuria) is derived, not by a simple filtration from the blood-vessels, but by the affinity or demand for the albumen of the blood by the continuous formation of imperfect or abortive cells, which either secrete it or produce it by their disintegration or breaking up.

Analogy is not proof; and thus far, I have only sought to show by analogy what happens in other tissues and in other diseases.

I shall be asked, can any direct observation or experiment be brought forward to justify the opinion that the albumen in morbus Brightii is derived from the breaking up of the abortive cellular elements of the uriniferous tubes?

It is a well-known pathological fact, that the contents of all cells are albuminous. The contents of the pus-cell are albuminous; the contents of the mucous or abortive epithelial-cell are albuminous.

Dr. William Addison, whose contributions to the doctrines of cellular pathology are well known in his work on ' Healthy and Diseased Structure,' says, " when blood- or pus-cells are ruptured by liquor potassæ, the resulting material is a viscous matter, apparently identical in all essential respects with lymph or mucus, capable of forming fibres; sometimes spontaneously, and always upon the application of re-agents, leaving an albuminous material in solution.

The pus-cell is admitted to be derived as a transitional form from other cellular elements, and especially from epithelial elements.

Now, if we take a number of pus-cells and act upon the cell-wall by liquor potassæ, the wall is dissolved, and the contents of the cell set free. If the viscid magma thus formed be acidulated with nitric acid to neutralize the potash, which holds the albumen in solution, upon the application of heat, or any of the known re-agents for albumen, the presence of that substance may clearly be demonstrated.

The inference I venture to draw from this experiment is, that the breaking up of the cell-wall by liquor potassæ has liberated the albuminous contents of the cells, while the miscroscope testifies to the disruption of the other elements of the tissue.

Objections no doubt may be advanced to the conclusion I would deduce from this experiment, but the subject is worthy of a more extended inquiry which I am at present pursuing. I would, however, venture here to offer as a subject for further inquiry—whether the albumen in the urine, in all cases where its presence is shown, is a secretion derived from the action of imperfect gland-cells; and if that question shall hereafter be satisfactorily answered in the affirmative; then, as a subsidiary subject of inquiry, I would venture to ask, is the albumen, a pathological substitute for urea, and if so, to what extent?

Several chemists have asserted that albumen can be converted into urea by the influence of certain oxidizing agents.

Bèchamp obtained urea by the action of permanganate of potash on albumen.

Dr. Lionel Beale states* that he has not been able to confirm these observations. On the other hand, Dr. Thudichum distinctly states† that when albumen is digested with permanganate of potash, urea is the result of the oxidation.

The chemical evidence is thus far contradictory; but the fact cannot have escaped notice, that cases frequently occur

* 'On the Urine,' p. 88.   † 'On the Pathology of the Urine,' p. 219.

in which the urine continues for months, and even years, persistently albuminous. I know two cases of near four years' duration, the patients' health being fairly re-established, all the chief functions being performed with undeviating regularity, and with no obvious disorder, except in the composition of the urine. The character of this being the presence of albumen, with diminution of urea. Although we are as yet without proof, yet it has appeared to me probable that the albumen in the urine (in these long standing cases) must, in some way, take the place of the urea, and become, as it were, its pathological substitute.

The organic chemists are very skilful in conjugating the elements of organic substances; or, in other words, transposing the elements of organic substances with the addition of an atom or two of oxygen, or an atom or two of the elements of water, of carbonic acid, or other proximate principles, and thus explaining the metamorphosis which a particular substance undergoes in the process of change. But there is, at present, no generally accepted formula for albumen, and, therefore, we cannot theoretically explain the probable conversion of albumen into urea by an oxidizing agent.

I am fully conscious that objections to the proposition that the albumen is a secretion derived from abortive or imperfect gland-cells, may be found in the cases of temporary albuminuria, apparently dependent on arrest of blood through the lungs producing a mechanical engorgement of the kidneys from obstruction to the current of blood from these organs, as in pneumonia, some forms of heart disease; the pressure in some cases of the gravid uterus, and in the experiment of Dr. Robinson of Newcastle, in tying the emulgent

veins in rabbits.* But the albumen in each of these instances finds its way into the urine as the result of simple
blood stasis in the kidney; from mechanical impediment to
the circulation. And I would venture to answer, that though
these be instances of temporary albuminuria, ceasing as soon
as the healthy current of the blood through the organs is
restored, yet even that temporary embarrassment of the
circulation is of sufficient duration to affect the healthy
development of the gland-cell. The moment the circulation through an organ is in any degree obstructed, provided
the obstruction be something more than momentary, the
function, the secretion, the nutrition, and consequently the
subsequent development of the gland-cells, is proportionately
disturbed.

Principles of Treatment.

I will now proceed to offer a few observations on the subject of treatment, and especially the principle which seems
to me more particularly applicable in these cases of renal
dropsy.

It has been shown that the disease is not limited to the
kidneys, that it is wide-spread in its influence, although the
focus of its devastation may be chiefly viewed in those
organs. It is essentially a process significant of deterioration and decay.

It must be admitted, that in the early history of these disorders, by far too exclusive attention has been paid to the
state of the kidneys and the urine; and, although this con-

* ' Med.-Chir. Trans.'

dition is manifestly the key to interpret the character of
the general disorder, yet remedies have been, and even continue to be given, having special reference to those organs,
and those organs only.

In the early acute stage of the disorder, at a period when
a tumultuous and destructive change is hurrying toward a
fatal issue, remedies are chiefly selected to control the local
process in the kidneys.

A distinguished physician and well-known writer on this
disease (Dr. Christison), recommends strongly, and practises
bloodletting in the acute stage, to moderate the inflammatory
action in these organs.

Other physicians prefer local depletion from the loins, either
by taking blood, or simply applying the cups.

Diaphoretics are employed to excite the action of the skin
and save the kidneys; drastic purgatives, at the same time,
to drain away the dropsical fluids, and husband the power of
the kidneys.

Digitalis to lower and moderate the heart's action, and by
its diuretic action increase the outlet of fluid by the kidneys.

Tannin and gallic acid to restrain and moderate the
drain of albumen by the kidneys, and uvæ ursi for a like
reason.

With the exception of bloodletting, each of the above-
named remedies may, according to the requirements of an
individual case, be needed, particularly in the early or acute
stage. Special symptoms will obviously require special remedies. But I am not dealing with the differences of individual
cases, for, as regards them, each case of morbus Brightii
affords a separate study; but I am desirous of drawing attention to that which is common to all—the unmistakable evi-

dence that this form of disease represents a degeneration or decay. It is not a state to be represented by the organism *plus* something which has to be taken away, but by the organism *minus* something which has to be added. Now that something is nutrition—nutritive elements of the nitrogenous series to supply the pabulum for fresh cells and active reproduction. Will bloodletting supply this? Will the abstraction of blood-globules from a fluid already exhausted of these, and reduced to a minimum, give aid to renewed cell-growth? In the acute form of the disease I do not affirm that diaphoretics are not needful. I do not affirm that purgatives are not often most salutary in reducing the amount of fluid accumulated in the tissues. I do not say that digitalis is not a most efficient agent in certain stages of these disorders; but I do say that they are each and all insufficient—positively harmful, if not accompanied or followed, according to their action, by agents and remedies intended to fulfil the fundamental principle of treatment, the restoration to the organism of the power of reproduction of those cells which are rapidly disappearing by processes of solution and decay.

With regard to bloodletting, I unhesitatingly assert that it is injurious: it is manifestly hostile to the fundamental principle on which the treatment of these forms of disease should be based. So long as these disorders were considered as inflammatory, so long as the dropsy was viewed as a product of inflammatory action, such treatment by venesection, or cupping, was only consistent with those doctrines. But here are forms of diseased action in which the blood itself exhibits a deficiency of its most important constituent, in which to take more blood would be but to deteriorate still more the

quality of the already impoverished fluid. The œdematous
eye-lids, the anasarcous extremities, the pasty, putty-like com-
plexion, the wheezing respiration from pulmonary œdema—
even though the albuminous urine be stained or tinged
with blood, and hæmaturia of notable amount has been
present, — signify deterioration, and decay ; a depraved
blood—broken down by some imperfect source of supply—
or poisoned by the presence of some of the so-called blood-
poisons, more especially the poison of scarlet fever, the
deleterious influence of which upon the blood few will dispute, although the manner of action is yet unknown.

If we suppose the blood of the patient in acute rheumatism, or of puerperal peritonitis, to represent the most
expressive form of inflammatory blood—blood characterised
by the excess of the fibrine and increase in the blood-
globules—a true *hyperinosis*—then the blood of albuminuria
stands as its very opposite—deficient in fibrine and blood
globules, a veritable *hypinosis*. If these views be correct—
if these pathological doctrines be admitted—then, *theoretically*, would not bloodletting be injurious? I have only to
appeal to those around me, to the experience of all physicians, and they will affirm that, *practically*, it is equally so.

If, then, the principle on which these cases of albuminuria
is to be conducted be to build up and restore, rather than to
take from or reduce, how and by what agents can this be
accomplished?

Rest, warmth, nutritive stimuli, and blood-forming remedies (hæmatics), are the agents by which this object may be
accomplished.

The very instincts, the necessity of the patient, will seek
rest, so far as rest means bodily quiet : but therapeutically

by rest is meant something more—it is an endeavour to place all the functions of the body in a comparative state of calm, to limit the excessive action of some and bring all, so far as may be placed in our power, to what may be called the physiological state of equilibrium and repose.

This will, of course, necessitate attention to those functions which are most disturbed, and which are most readily within the reach of medicinal agents. It is, therefore, at this stage, that the action of diaphoretics and purgatives and even hydrogogue cathartics may be necessary. These latter are often productive of great benefit, by draining from the system, through their action on the intestinal villi, the serous fluid which infiltrates the tissues, and which the kidneys are totally unable to excrete. The glandular function of the kidneys is for a time in abeyance, the epithelial-cells are cloudy with granular matter, which is either infiltrating the interstitial tissue of the kidney, or the cells are cast forth in tubular masses, abortive and inefficient. A drain of fluid by the intestines, relieves to a certain extent the kidneys; and it is a well known clinical fact that in all those cases of renal dropsy in which diarrhœa occurs spontaneously, a more favorable progress is noted, than in those where the same result has to be obtained by drastic purgatives.

At this early stage of the disorder we find those differences in the degree and character of the functional disturbances, other than the renal, which renders it impossible to lay down any unalterable scheme for our guidance. Every case in this respect is a study of itself.

If it be borne in mind, that the sole object of the physician in the management of a case of renal dropsy at the earlier period, is to prepare the organism for the influence of

4

the nutritive stimuli and blood forming remedies which
constitute the fundamental measures of cure, then it will be
needless to expatiate further on the various remedies which
may appropriately enough be employed in this preparatory
stage of treatment. A detail of the treatment of the early
period, or what is called the acute stage of the disease, is
unnecessary, as my object is to consider rather the principle
which is to guide us in the treatment of the case which has
passed from the acute to the chronic stage, and presents
some favorable indications of relief.

Warmth is in itself so essential an element of nutrition,
that it is only necessary for me to observe here, that a careful
attention to maintain the surface of the body at an equable
state of temperature by means of flannel clothing, and in the
winter time by avoiding an exposure to irregularity of cold,
are advantages which cannot be over estimated in the management of renal dropsy.

The influence of pure air, the stimulus given to the blood
forming power by the agency of pure air, is too well known
to require further remark. In the management of cases
in a rank of life where change of residence can be com-
manded, the sea-side, or resort to localities elevated in
situation, and possessing the characters of what is called a
bracing quality, should be selected. But these are points
which need no further comment.

I turn, however, to what may be called nutritive stimulants.

I feel now, sir, that I am entering on controversial ground.
The consideration of the action of stimulants in renal dropsy
opens up the whole question, whether alcohol is a nutritive
element or not.

The limit of these lectures will not permit me to enter into the fulness of this question, so interesting to the practical physician. The subject has been discussed from a chemical point of view, as well as from a physiological one.

I will venture to look at it simply from the clinical point of view without committing myself to the declaration, that wine or alcohol is a nutriment. I will venture, nevertheless, to assert that clinical observation proves it a most efficient (hand-maid) aid to nutritives.

From the clinical point of view it is generally believed that in most diseases, especially those of a low and depressed character, that the elements of nutrition are more energetically and efficiently taken up and appropriated by the aid of vinous stimuli than without them.

Clinically the result is, I believe, beyond dispute. But, can the beneficial effect of this agent be theoretically explained?

It would be out of place here, and beyond the purport and scope of these lectures, to discuss the question of the action of alcohol. But, I trust an observation on the use of vinous stimuli in renal dropsy may not be thought inappropriate.

In considering the use of vinous stimuli in renal dropsy, I would most emphatically place certain limits on its use.

First, as regards the quality or kind, as well as the amount or quantity, and *time* for use.

Secondly, as to the stage of the disease in which it is most efficient.

First, as to the quality or kind. All crude spirits derived from the distillation of grain or sugar are prejudicial; they are certainly not equally efficacious with those derived by fermentation from the grape. Brandy, whiskey, hollands, gin, rum, are prejudicial, even beer is of doubtful use. The stimulants most beneficial are wines of any kind, or country, provided they are pure and sound. They must be used in moderate quantity, and always in conjunction with food, particularly animal food, either at, or immediately after the meal. They must, on no account, be taken on an empty stomach. Wines thus given appear to promote the digestion of nitrogenous substances; to invigorate the metamorphosis of the products of digestion; and to enrich the blood with material calculated to promote cell growth. Moreover, wine in moderation, increases the chief constituent of the urine, urea; and, if this be derived from the metamorphosis of the muscular elements, it would directly show that a larger amount of nitrogenous food was appropriated, and that nutrition had become more active.

We are taught physiologically that wine diminishes the quantity of urea, for it saves tissue, and urea is derived from the metamorphosis of muscular tissue; but I would infer clinically, that wine, by promoting the digestion of nitrogenous food, increases the urea, though diminishing the amount of the metamorphosis of the tissues of the body.

The stage of the disease best calculated to feel the beneficial influence of wine is not so difficult to determine as at first might be imagined.

I believe it will be found, that except during the very commencement of the symptoms, when to the evidence of engorgement of the kidneys, through the presence of hæmaturia, there are added some degree of febrile disturbance, restlessness, thirst, inappetency, and a furred tongue, that, under every other condition of the patient, wine in moderation should be prescribed. The instant the stomach will bear animal food, or, in other words, as soon as the inclination of the patient permits it, animal food should be given in some palatable form, and its amount thereafter proportioned to the powers of the patient's digestion. At first beef-tea, or some well prepared soup is all that the stomach can, without disturbance, digest; but slowly and gradually the stomach recovers its power, and the patient begins to crave for more.

It is a most interesting fact to remark here, that the albumen in the urine *decreases* by the use of animal food, and *increases* again under a vegetable diet. I have experimentally proved this. Is it not natural then to conclude, that the nitrogenous elements of animal food are better adapted to enrich the blood with the elements of cell-forming power in these diseases where that power is deficient, than can be expected or gained from any form of vegetable diet?

But animal food, even with improved powers of digestion, though aided by wine, will but slowly impart to the impoverished and watery blood, the nutritive material necessary for its restoration, to fit it, in its turn, for the support and nutrition of the tissues.

The preparations of iron have long been justly regarded as instrumental in helping to enrich the blood with red corpuscles; and hence appropriately enough called hæmatics. In all cases where there is evidence of a poor defective blood, called by whatsoever name, anæmia, spanæmia, leukæmia, in the sequel of many acute diseases, whether as the result of treatment by bleeding, as was formerly the case in acute rheumatic fever, or from the blood-destroying character of the disease itself, as in the convalescing stage of most fevers,

whether continued or intermittent, the rapid and beneficial
restorative action of chalybeate medicines or steel, as it is
popularly called, particularly in conjunction with animal
food and wine, is universally acknowledged and confirmed
by daily experience. The preparations of iron in the 'Pharmacopœia' are numerous, but there is one which in these
cases of renal dropsy stands pre-eminent for its efficacy, and
should be preferred in these cases before all others. It is
the tincture of the sesquichloride. But it is not as a sesquichloride that its efficacy is most perceived in these cases.
It is as an ammonio-chloride, kept in solution by acetic acid,
that its beneficial influence becomes most apparent. It is a
very simple preparation, a few drops of the tincture, according to the age of the patient, are added to a dram of the
liquor ammonia acetatis, previously acidulated with acetic
acid.

If this be not done—if the sesquichloride is added to the
neutral liquor, an insoluble ammonio-chloride falls, which is
with difficulty again taken up; but, if the saline is first acidulated a beautiful sherry-red fluid is produced, which is neither
unpalatable, nor liable to decomposition, and may be kept any
time.   The tincture of the sesquichloride has long possessed
the favorable opinion of physicians in most cases of renal or
genito-vesical disorder.

It has been supposed to act almost specifically in dysuria
from spasmodic conditions of the sphincter of the neck of the
bladder. Dr. Parkes, in his excellent work on the Urine, p. 395,
thinks that the sesquichloride in morbus Brightii, reduces the
quantity of water, and probably, in some instances, the albumen.   So far, however, as my observations enable me to
judge, these conditions, more particularly the diminution of

the albumen, or the alteration of its chemical character, that is, its conversion into the condition of albuminose, a modified albumen, does not become evident till proofs are equally present by the diminution or disappearance of the dropsy, and the altered character of the cells and casts thrown off from the kidneys, that a blood, richer in all the elements of cell-growth, has been produced.

It has fallen under my observation that in the long period which elapses while these beneficial results are progressing, that the albumen thrown off with the urine undergoes certain modifications, and passes from the ordinary condition, so familiar to us as coagulating by heat and nitric acid, into one which the chemists have called albuminose, or modified albumen, and which has been regarded as an oxidized form of albumen, and called the deutoxide of albumen. I think that when it is discovered that the albuminous product has undergone this change a more favorable opinion may be expressed as to ultimate and permanent recovery, than where, notwithstanding the disappearance of the dropsy and the general improvement in the health of the patient, the urine continues to exhibit, although in decreasing quantity, the presence of albumen in its ordinary form.

Time will not permit my giving in detail the history of cases which illustrate the favorable progress that may be expected to follow the steady adhesion to these principles of treatment. I can refer to several cases of three and four years', and one of seven years' duration. The interest attaching to these cases consists in the steady improvement of the general health, notwithstanding the daily drain, during more than three years of a large amount of albumen, an improvement which has steadily proceeded with concurring

evidence of the gradual restoration of healthy cell development. These beneficial results appear to me to have been
brought about by an undeviating, unhesitating course of
treatment based on the principles set before you—commencing at a time when the patient's condition was most
unpromising, and continued with but partial interruptions,
and those but for a few days, up to the present time.

General Reflections on the preceding.

I well venture, then, to conclude that renal dropsy—dropsy
with albuminous urine—is significant not only of various
forms and degrees of kidney degeneration, but of a decadence
and consequent failure in function of almost all the other
tissues of the body. It would appear to be significant of a
wide and all but universal defect in the formative or cell
forming agency.

If we adopt the physiological view, that healthy cell development depends on the selection of highly nitrogenized material for the nucleus, as well as for the contents of the cell,
that cell representing the highest degree of vital activity
and energy in which the nitrogenous nucleus is the most
concentrated ; then viewing the development of less healthy
cells, the power of selecting or condensing nitrogenous
matter grows weaker and weaker, till in the lowest forms
the cell contains but an albuminous fluid with hydrocarbon
granules, oftentimes fatty, perhaps amyloid, and consequently totally inefficient for all functional purposes of
secretion.

From this point of view I will venture to submit that our

methods of treatment should more decidedly embrace the principle of nutrition and support; that our main object should be to invigorate the powers of the organism; that we should call to our aid whatever is calculated to maintain and promote the force of cellular reproduction, so that, by these means, the decaying powers may, if possible, be revived.

Guided by such principles, many cases which at first afford but faint prospect of relief, pass from a stage of imminent danger to one of hope and encouragement; and eventually either permanently recover, or at least give assurance that a form of disease which was but lately thought incurable may be brought within the category of those which are remediable and tractable.

LECTURE III.

MR. PRESIDENT AND GENTLEMEN,—I desire to-day to ask your attention to some pathological facts connected with cardiac and pulmonary dropsy.

Dropsy is significant of two forms of disease of the heart. In one, the affection of the heart is viewed as the primary cause of the dropsy. In the other, the condition of the heart is secondary or subsidiary to certain states of the lungs.

It is to these two forms of heart disease connected with dropsy that I desire now to direct attention.

In the first of these, the disease originates in the heart; the left heart, more particularly its valves. In the second, the heart becomes implicated as a sequel to disease in other organs, more particularly the lungs, with evidence of defective nutrition in itself. In the first case, therefore, the heart is the primary source of the symptoms; in the second, it is only subordinate or intermediate thereto.

As a preface to the subject of cardiac dropsy, perhaps I may be permitted to place before you, by way of contrast, two typical cases of this form of disease; the one arising from mitral regurgitant and aortic obstructive disease; the other originating in emphysema and chronic bronchitis, and mani-

festing changes in the right heart, in the shape of dilatation
and attenuation of its walls.

A young person, about the age of puberty, has suffered
from symptoms of acute rheumatic fever; the cardiac complications may have been pericarditis, or disorganization of
the mitral and aortic valves. The convalescence from the
fever is slow, and probably marked by shortness of breath
and great palpitations on the slightest bodily effort; a few
weeks pass; some ill-defined disturbing cause occurs.; the
respirations become more deeply affected; and soon the feet
and ankles begin to swell. There is a remarkable alabaster
whiteness of the skin. The dropsy rises higher and higher;
the cutaneous surface glistens from over distension. The
heart's action becomes more and more embarrassed and
tumultuous; the lungs become gorged. There is a frequent
short and distressing cough. The sputa are frothy and blood-
stained; the breath is cold. The impulse of the heart to the
hand is undulatory, and a confused systolic murmur is heard;
fine moist crepitating sounds are heard all over the chest, and
more particularly at the base of both lungs. The eye-balls
are protruding. The alæ nasi are distended, and rise and
fall during the hurried and laboured respiration. The
youthful countenance has an anxious and remarkable expression, given by the glistening sclerotic. The tongue is red
and moist; purplish perhaps, but clean, or moist and clammy.
The urine is scanty, but free from albumen. The abdominal
cavity is also free from fluid; or, perhaps slowly, signs of
its presence may come on from imperfect circulation through
the liver. The respirations become more frequent, more
laboured, more distressing. The tubes of the air-passages
fill with frothy sputa from the gorged lungs, and soon the

scene closes, and death by apnœa terminates the sufferings of
the youthful patient.

Such is the significant picture of dropsy from disease of
the left heart—essentially cardiac dropsy.

Let me ask attention to the characteristics of the other
forms of dropsy, where the heart becomes secondarily
affected.

A person of the middle period of life has long been sub-
jected to chronic cough and occasional attacks of dyspnœa, with
more or less abundant expectoration.

The health begins to fail; to break as the people say.
The feet begin to swell, and bodily activity gradually becomes more and more limited. The dropsical effusion increases and extends. The cough and shortness of breath become more distressing. There are frequent, even daily attacks
of a spasmodic gasping for breath, and the inspiratory movement of the chest is reduced to the minimum limit.

The countenance wears a dull, leaden expression; the
face becomes dusky; the eyes inexpressive, hazy and misty
in their character. The lips are bluish; the tongue cold,
clammy, and of a livid hue. The breath comes to the
hand reduced in temperature. The upper and lower extremities become more and more anasarcous; and the feet and
hands are bluish and mottled. A distressing tension of the
cuticle, even to bursting, marks also the extent of the infiltration of the connective tissue of the extremities, and in
colour and temperature they may assimilate the appearance
of mortification.

The abdomen may afford, by fluctuation, signs of the
presence of fluid; and the urine, scanty and high coloured,
may begin to exhibit traces of albumen.

The patient is propped up in bed, bent forward; the shoulders rounded, so that the head may be bowed between the knees.

An exalted resonance characterises the percussion sound of the chest behind; no ordinary respiratory sound can be heard; a moist or coarse mucous murmur, with wheezing and cooing sounds are heard everywhere.

The heart affords the feeblest impulse; perhaps none can be felt; the first and second sounds are distinct; perhaps sharper than natural. There is a remarkable pulsation observed in the veins of the neck.

The patient, propped up in bed, dozes rather than sleeps; takes food scantily; for either there is no desire for it, or so much flatulence follows, that a dread of the increased oppression to the breathing which follows, increases the aversion to it.

Such are the most distinctive features of that form of cardiac dropsy which arises from passive dilatation of the right heart; this organ, however, being secondarily, and not primarily affected, as in the first-named typical case.

The first of these disorders has reference to the valvular structures of the left side of the heart.

The second relates chiefly to the state of the walls, and the capacity of the cavities of the right side.

Moreover, as further points of distinction, the first is traceable, for the most part, to antecedent acute rheumatic inflammation, when the endocardium, the valves of the left cavity, or the pericardium, have been the seat of rheumatic disturbance, while the second has its origin in pulmonary disorder of long standing duration.

Disorganization of the valves of the left side of the heart

is a well known concomitant of acute rheumatism; yet it is
not a little remarkable, and must be familiar to most physicians, how few suffer from dropsy, of those whose mitral
valves only have become disordered; and in whom a mitral
murmur is easily detected. How many patients we meet
with who for years have thus suffered from an imperfect
mitral valve, who enjoy a fair share of health, and who,
except that they are not equal to any rapid bodily effort,
such as running, or being hurried in their movements, go
through a life of average duration without other serious
inconvenience.

This exemption from the serious evils which follow a like
form of disease in others, is partly due, perhaps, to the extent
of the disorganization of the mitral valve, which will, of course,
regulate the amount of pulmonary disturbance that will
follow; but partly, and I believe chiefly, to the character of the
succeeding changes which may occur in the morbid deposit
leading to the disorganization of the valves.

The degree and extent of the deposit, whatever its character, must of course be the measure of the pulmonary disturbance, so that when the mitral valve is simply thickened,
or its margin irregular, permitting a moderate amount of
regurgitation, there will be a very different degree of pulmonary embarrassment, as compared with those cases in which
both mitral and aortic valves are implicated, and where there
is both aortic obstruction, as well as aortic and mitral regurgitant disorder; but it is chiefly to the special pathological character and resulting changes which take place in
the deposit, that we must look for an explanation of the comparative immunity of some patients from serious and fatal
consequences, and the fatality attending the disorder in others.

Hitherto it has been conceived that these deposits on the valves are derived directly as an exudation from the blood; in fact, a transudation, a filtrate of fibrine (from the hyperinotic blood) through the walls of the capillary vessels, and a simple permeation through the serous coat of the endocardium, and a deposit as coagulated fibrine on the surface of the valves. But I think Virchow ('Cellular Pathology,' p. 363, by Chance) has conclusively shown that there is no exudation in the sense formerly conceived; but that the cellular elements of the endocardial membrane take up a greater quantity of material, and the spot becomes swollen, and eventually rugged excrescences, or condyloma arise, and the integrity of the valve is destroyed.

Now, this deposit always exhibits a fibriform character when examined with the microscope:—if recent, it displays appearances somewhat dissimilar to fleshly coagulated fibrine, wavy or sinuous lines interlacing each other with more or less granular matter entangled in the meshes.

This deposit appears to suffer, or to develope within itself, different results. In some cases the morbid process seems to run a very rapid and tumultuous course; the fibriform deposit softens and crumbles down, drops off the valves to which it has been but loosely attached, is carried into the circulation, and those embolic deposits in remote and distant organs are produced with which we are now familiar; results made known to us, however, by Virchow, and subsequently by Dr. Kirkes, about the same time as by Virchow.

But there are two other resulting changes which these deposits undergo, and which are more particularly connected with the subject before me.

First, there is established a subordinate metamorphosis of
the material deposited, a slow and continuous calcificative
change takes place apparently in certain central or dis-
severed points, and inorganic elements first in small, and
eventually in larger quantities, can be chemically demonstrated. The inorganic material is always carbonate and
phosphate of lime, in the same relative proportion as they
are found in bone. There can frequently be demonstrated
an obscure disposition to a stellar form of arrangement in the
inorganic deposit, analogous to the stellate-cells of bone,
which I conceive can only be effected through the agency of
cells. This change in the character of the deposit has
appropriately enough been termed the calcifying process.
(Plate V, figs. 1 and 2.) It is a degree less than the process of ossification. Calcification appears to be to these
cardiac and valvular deposits what cretefication is to tubercle.
The term cretefication is inappropriate, for the earthy matter,
the conservative metamorphosis of pulmonary tubercle, is not
chalk ; but carbonate and phosphate of lime in similar proportion to what exists in bone; and is, therefore, a strictly
analogous process to that of calcification of cardiac and arterial
tissue. (A specimen of cretefied tubercle is on the table.)

To return to the subordinate metamorphosis which takes
place in these endocardial deposits.

The granular material, of which the deposit appears originally composed presents a certain wavy undulatory arrangement of the accompanying fibres, and gradually takes up
earthy material at isolated points; these seem incapable of
further change, except that which relates to extent and
quantity.

It is this calcifying process which renders the deposit in-

capable of further change, and is assumed to exist in the
valves of those who carry through life a systolic mitral
murmur, and whose health does not materially suffer from
its presence. It has occurred to me within the last five
years to make a post-mortem examination of two persons
who died from fever, who were known to have suffered
severally, the one for eight, the other for twelve years, from
a well pronounced mitral murmur. In both of these the
margin of the mitral valve was opaque, and presented the
character of a rigid ring, and cut with a grating sound; the
left ventricle was hypertrophic. In both of these the earthy
deposit existed, as shown in these drawings ; and its chemical
constitution was verified by analysis. (Plate V, figs. 1
and 2.) I assume, then, that this is the condition which
ensures comparative safety to the patient from the ulterior
effects of a disorganized valve; and explains, I think satisfactorily, the reason for this immunity.

There is one condition which must not be overlooked, and
which may exercise a commanding influence over these
favorable results : the body continues well nourished, and
cell-development we may believe continues vigorous, healthy,
and active.

The thickening of the valves in these cases originally
arises from an excess of a fine granular matter, usually
considered as arising from an inflammatory process, which is
deposited in the texture of the valve.

It is really a thickening of the structural elements of the
endocardial membrane which appear to take up this granular
product and retains it ; and it is in this granular material
that minute traces of earthy matter may be traced. Microscopically, the tissue appears composed of wavy sinuous lines,

5

with a very granular aspect, studded here and there with
patches of a dark, almost black aspect, which arises from
light not being transmitted through them; by reflected light
they appear white. The dark spots are quickly removed by
digestion in dilute hydrochloric acid, and the solution yields
by analysis proofs of the presence of carbonate and phosphate
of lime.

This then, is the form of valvular disorder which remains
so comparatively inert, or which at any rate, exhibits no
disposition to be followed by dropsical symptoms.

The most frequent result is hypertrophy, or increased
nutrition of the walls of the left ventricle, with the probable
consequences of that complication. It is rarely, I believe
never, the starting-point of cardiac dropsy.

The significance, then, of this process of calcification of the
valve is not dropsy. Its morbid results and sequel are, for
the most part, in an opposite direction. It may be, and
most frequently is, followed by apoplexy; and I think we
may here find an explanation of that pathological view which
brings apoplexy in direct relation to hypertrophy of the
heart. They have been placed in the position of cause and
effect. The cerebral hæmorrhage in apoplexy has been
made to depend directly on the increased driving power of
a strong and hypertrophic ventricle. But that which laid
the foundation for the increased nutrition and strength of its
walls, the morbid deposit forming the organic defect in
the valve, becomes the immediate cause of the apoplexy.

That which most usually originates hypertrophy of the
left heart, is either an imperfection of the valvular apparatus
of this side, or a slowly increasing rigidity, and defective
elasticity of the aortic sinus caused by deposits of an opaque

material, commonly called atheroma. (Plate V, fig. 1.) In cases of hypertrophy of the heart from these causes, this pathological product is not confined to the endocardial or aortic tissues; but slowly extends through the arterial system generally, and is either more abundantly deposited in the cerebral arteries, or their elasticity is more fatally destroyed. (Plate V, fig. 3.)

The brittleness or loss of elasticity in process of time arrives at that point that, under excitement of some disturbing cause, emotional or physical, the vessels, unequal to the increased pressure of blood from a powerful driving force on one side, and the impediment to the escape of blood through the great venous outlets, which is produced by the constriction the jugulars suffer by the muscles of the neck, whether from emotional or physical causes, give way, and hæmorrhage into the cerebral substance, or apoplexy follows.

I have already pointed out the disposition which is apparent in this process of calcification for the earthy matter—obscurely in some cases, but, in cases of the so-called ossification of arteries, more pointedly, to assume the stellate form of arrangement, such as is apparent in ordinary osseous structures. I cannot conceive that this disposition to such a symmetrical grouping of the earthy matter can result from mere molecular attraction; but I believe it to be regulated by the organic or cellular elements in which the process is taking place.

I shall presently have occasion to refer more particularly to the agency of the cellular elements of these textures, after I have noticed the other form of subsidiary change and metamorphosis which these deposits suffer, and which becomes significant of the dropsy which follows. This, sad to say, is by far the most frequent sequel to these valvular disorders.

As in the calcifying process, so in this, the changes are slow, insidious; and but for some attending symptoms to be noticed hereafter, only indirectly to be predicted during life.

This process is essentially a fatty degeneration of the morbid deposit. Not only are large and highly refractive granules of fat generated throughout the deposit; but these evidences of degeneration are further accompanied by beautiful plates of cholesterine, most significantly conveying to us indisputable proof that the elements of this change are essentially fatty, and consequently a degenerative process. (Plate V, figs. 4 and 5.)

Here are two results of a fibrinous exudation to be considered, the one earthy, the other fatty. I will venture to ask, through what agency are these changes brought about? Are we to be satisfied with the bald statement, that some exudations undergo one change, others another?

If a fibrinous exudation undergoes liquefaction, and pus is formed, we do not hesitate to acknowledge that this change is brought about by the metamorphosis of its cellular elements.

If we take a fatty liver, the seat of fatty or amyloid degeneration, we can demonstrate that the fatty and amylaceous material is accumulated within the imperfect liver-cell.

If we examine a waxy kidney, one expressive of the highest degree of degeneration, we see that the cellular elements are highly charged with fat, and that what we see accumulated in the convoluted tubes, or deposited in the intertubular spaces, has been brought there through the agency of imperfect cell development.

May we not then conclude in these cardiac exudations, that the exudation contains cellular elements, as yet but obscurely demonstrated, which are prone to take up earthy matter in one case, or to undergo fatty metamorphosis in the other?

In other words, that the cellular elements of the spurious tissue, never reaching the elective force of true development, nevertheless, in one direction, indicate a conservative force, by the selection of the elements to form bone, which in some rare cases is partially reached, as in ossification of arteries, where not only a maximum amount of earthy matter is taken up, but where stellate cells are formed; and although this is not true bone, yet it indicates the disposition of the structural elements to work in the physiological rather than in the pathological direction.

Plate V, figs. 1 and 2, represent spots of calcification, indicating a disposition to a stellate form of deposit of the earthy material.

On the other hand, there is the direction of an opposite type, where the tendency is to pass downward, in the course of fatty decay. The cells are abortive, their nuclei are fatty; they soon disintegrate and perish, and they leave in the surrounding texture evidence of the extent to which this form of decay has reached.

These two subordinate changes are easily seen by the microscope in the opaque patches on and in the mitral valves; but it is also as easily recognised in the patches of atheroma, as they are called, which stud the commencement of the aorta, and, in many cases, can be detected in remoter parts of the arterial system.

In the form of fatty metamorphosis the valvular disorganisation is usually greater, both mitral and aortic valves being implicated; the disturbance to the equilibrium of the circulation is also more manifest than in the first-enumerated class, where so little inconvenience apparently results.

In studying, therefore, the dropsical condition as significant of cardiac disease, we must not only satisfy ourselves as to the amount of mechanical impediment to the free circulation of the blood through the lungs and heart, but we must also take into our estimate the correlative changes which are going on, not only in the morbid deposit on and in the valves, but also in the heart itself, as well as in other organs.

First. As to the mechanical impediment. This is too well understood to need either explanation or comment. The imperfections of both the mitral and aortic valves will represent the maximum degree of mechanical impediment which can oppose the current of blood through the heart; an imperfect mitral valve will, according to its degree, cause regurgitation into the left auricle, and embarrassment to the return of blood from the lungs; but an imperfection of the aortic valves may either consist in such a thickening as shall simply cause obstruction, or they may be disorganized so that complete closure is impossible, and not only obstructions to the flow of blood outward by the systole is the result, but a regurgitation of blood from the aortic sinus into the ventricle will be an additional impediment to the integrity of the heart's action.

In both these cases, differing only in degree, the patient suffers from pulmonary engorgement; and bronchitis, hæmoptysis, or pulmonary apoplexy, may severally follow. The extent to which the patient may thus suffer from the effects

of heart disease will sometimes be proportioned to the strain
laid upon the powers of the heart; and if physical rest and
exemption from bodily toil be enjoyed, and if the organism
continue well nourished, the heart—even thus disorganised—
will continue its functions, although imperfectly, without
giving rise to any symptoms of dropsy. But soon the ankles
and feet begin to swell, then the legs and thighs; tediously
and sluggishly the serous effusion increases; dyspnœa, even
without physical exertion, occurs; the lungs become œdematous also; the urine decreases in amount, step by step,
as the dropsical condition increases; cough and shortness
of breath become more urgent; coarse wheezing murmurs are
heard all over the chest; ascites sometimes supervenes; both
upper and lower extremities are anasarcous; the cuticle of
the legs is distended to the utmost; a painful erythematous
redness may be followed by vesications, which burst and
distil the serous infiltration of the tissues, and thus tempo-
rarily relieves the tension—or incisions, or scarifications are
employed to obtain a like result. There is no abatement of
the dropsy; the breathing becomes more embarrassed; and
either from increasing engorgement of the lungs, or what
may be thought an attack of broncho-pneumonia, the patient
sinks and dies.

I will venture to ask, is this frightful and all but invariably
unchecked dropsical accumulation significant only of mechanical impediment to the course of blood through the heart?
Are we to look for no other cause for this fatal issue than a
mechanical one? There has been throughout his sufferings
no *increase* in the mechanical obstacles—they have remained
throughout the same—and doubtless have ministered in
some degree, by the direct obstruction to the circulation,

to impede the return of blood through the right side of the
heart.

In fatal cases we have not to search far for abundant evidence that the mechanical conditions referred to in the heart
are invariably accompanied both in the structure of its
walls, as well as in other textures, by a decay and a
degeneration in the elements of the tissues, such as may be
demonstrated in renal dropsy. I would, with reference to
this part of my subject, venture to recall attention to my
observations on the state of the tissues in renal dropsy; but
I would merely repeat here that, as in that form of dropsy,
the morbid phenomena appear to express themselves most
significantly by disorder in the function and structure of the
kidneys, but are accompanied by unequivocal evidence of a
wide-spread deterioration of cell growth : so in this form of
dropsy, which appears to originate in a disorganization of the
valves of the heart, there is equally demonstrable a similar
state of decay and degeneration, not only in the muscular
walls of the heart, but also in the remotest tissues of the
organism.

To explain the mechanical development of dropsy from
disorganization of the left valves of the heart, it is usually
laid down as a rule that dropsical effusion does not take place
until the engorgement of the lungs has reached a point by
which the circulation or free movement of the blood through
the pulmonary artery is seriously embarrassed, and venous
retardation in the cavæ has brought about a condition analogous nearly to what we familiarly know to happen when the
circulation through a trunk vein is impeded, viz., a state of
serous effusion or œdema in all the tissues supplying venous
blood to that obstructed vein. Cardiac dropsy, even when

the left cavity of the heart is at fault, is supposed to be
generated by a series of retrograde effects or impediments
beginning in the left cavity of the heart, carried to the circulation through the lungs, imparted to the current through
the pulmonary artery, felt in the right ventricle, and thence
impeding the freedom of the venous circulation through
the cavæ, subsequently through the liver and abdominal
viscera, and ultimately through the entire venous system.
An obstruction or impediment to the freedom of the venous
circulation throughout the body is a very intelligible cause,
and is the one usually assigned to explain the accumulation
of fluid in dropsy from heart disease. But the mechanical
impediment has been the same from the beginning, and in
the beginning there was no dropsy. If the mechanical
conditions, the imperfection and disorganization of the
valves, were constantly increasing conditions, the impediment
through the heart constantly becoming greater, the mechanical interpretation might be sufficient. But the heart disease, when followed by dropsy, is invariably, and I believe
unexceptionally, followed by changes not only in the morbid
materials constituting the first stage of the disease, but by
analogous changes in cell growth elsewhere, by which the
tissues and cells are eventually rendered incapable of carrying
on the functions of health—even of life.

I have yet the other form of heart disease of which dropsy
is significant to mention; and I would desire to postpone
laying before you the evidence of this wide-spread cell
deterioration, which occurs equally in both forms, till I have
sketched the general character and progress of this second
variety, since what in cellular deterioration is characteristic of
one is also pointedly significant of the other.

The other form of heart disease of which dropsy is significant must be considered as a passive rather than an active
disorder; it is secondary and subordinate to disturbances
and diseases of other organs. The heart condition is, therefore, intermediate and resultant, not primary nor inceptive.

The relation of emphysema and chronic bronchitis to dilatation of the right side of the heart is a pathological connection too familiar to render necessary more than a passing
observation.

If we attentively examine the pathological conditions
of emphysema (the emphysema lobulare of authors, Roki-
tansky and others), we shall without difficulty, recognise in it
one of the most efficient causes for embarrassment to the
circulation of blood through the right side of the heart.

The disease (emphysema) is essentially a dilatation of
the pulmonary air-cell, or two or more cells may become
blended in one—the elastic or expansive power of the cell is
destroyed—it becomes a passive undilatable vesicle; the vascular layer, distributed to the parenchymatous surface of the
cell, becomes obliterated—atrophied—and is no longer the
instrument of circulation, and these pulmonary cells are
completely cut off from all office of aërating (oxygenating)
the blood. In post-mortem examinations we see these air-
cells like colourless dilated vesicles on the surface of the
tissue. That the capillaries are occluded is proved by the
fact that no injection, not even the finest, will reach them. I
have, in more than one instance, seen with the microscope
the blood-vessels leading to an emphysematous portion of
lung in a state of fatty granular decay. (Plate VI, fig. 5.)

I believe that both the dilatation of these pulmonary cells,
and the atrophy of the vascular walls of the capillaries,

originate in a granular and fatty degeneration of these textures.

It is beyond the scope and purport of these lectures to enter upon an inquiry into the *origin* or cause of emphysema. There is the inspiratory theory and the expiratory theory; however produced, there must be an antecedent *predisposing state*, a morbid predisposition of the tissue to suffer and lose its elasticity, and become inert for the purpose of respiration. From examination I have made of emphysematous lungs, I have always found the sero-fibrous structure of the dilated air-cells granular, and studded with highly refractive fat-granules. (Plate VI, figs. 1 and 2.)

So far back as 1848, Mr. Rainey communicated to the Royal Medical and Chirurgical Society a paper on " The Emphysematous Lung,"* in which he distinctly showed that a fatty degeneration of the fibro-serous elements of the air-cell was the obvious condition of emphysema; and he sums up a most excellent paper by stating that the form of emphysema he describes originates in a morbid process going on in the pulmonary membrane, which is essentially a fatty degeneration.

It is remarkable that the subject of the degeneration of pulmonary tissues in emphysema and chronic bronchitis has received but little notice since that date.

This passing reference to the pathology of emphysema will, I think, exhibit intelligibly enough the agency of this state of lung in conducing to embarrassment in the pulmonary circulation, and impediment to the flow of blood through the right side of the heart.

* Vol. xxxi, p. 300.

In like manner, although not always with the same rapidity, will chronic bronchitis, especially if it be of long standing and associated with bronchicctasis, or dilatation of the
bronchial tubes, bring about the same embarrassment in the
pulmonary circulation, and a similar obstruction to the
flow of blood through the pulmonary artery.

Plate VI, fig. 2, represents the bronchial textures in emphysema and chronic bronchitis. There is very little difference to be noted in either form of disease, so far as the
bronchial tubes are concerned. In both, the protective
layer of ciliated epithelium is gone, and the succeeding layers
of cells are all of the depraved type of mucous, or even pus-
cells. The fibro-elastic layer, as well as the unstriped muscular layer, are both fatty, though not to so great an extent,
as may be seen in some cases of morbus Brightii.

The drawing was made from strongly marked typical cases
of emphysema and chronic bronchitis, with succeeding dropsy.
I have found the same appearances in every case I have examined. Emphysema and chronic bronchitis are so intimately connected the one with the other—the emphysematous
patient constantly suffering from bronchitis, acute or chronic,
and the lungs of the sufferer from chronic bronchitis so
often becoming emphysematous—that in relation to a state of
the heart, which is followed by dropsy, they may be taken as
identical.

In emphysema there is, proportioned to the wasting or
atrophy of the vascular element of the dilated pulmonary
cells, a deficiency in the capacity of the lungs for the recep-
tion of the blood from the right side of the heart. There
must also be taken into consideration a morbid condition,
or at least an increased susceptibility of the branches of the

eighth nerve distributed to the bronchial membrane and
non-striated muscular element.

Partly, then, from the limited area of the pulmonary circulation and a morbid susceptibility to disturbance of
the par vagum spasmodic attacks of difficulty of breathing,
and paroxysms of shortness of breath, occur.

The expansibility of the chest becomes narrowed to
the smallest limits, and unavailing and abortive inspiratory efforts, marked by the anxious expression of
countenance, the protruding eye-balls, the dull, even
dusky venosity of the features, the purplish lips, the
tongue turgid with venous blood, and the breath deficient
in warmth, severally proclaim the embarrassment which
the pulmonary circulation suffers. The heart's action becomes hurried and laboured; and unequal efforts are made to
drive the impeded venous blood through the pulmonary
artery. The action of the heart thus embarrassed continues
to labour with abortive efforts. Slowly, day by day, week
by week, and month by month, this overstrain continues;
occasionally interrupted by periods of calm and comparative
ease; but the current through the pulmonary artery, never
so free, even in these intervals of calm as it ought to be,
continues to oppress and exact the driving power of the
right side; gradually and sluggishly the walls of the cavity
yield to a passive dilating power. As the dilatation increases, the walls become more and more attenuated, till at
length the feebleness of the heart's contractility scarcely
suffices to drive the blood forward through the lung; general
venosity follows, and a diffuse dropsy, characterised not only
by anasarca of upper and lower extremities, but by a per-
sistent blueness or lividity of the lips, hands, and feet, mark-

ing in a most striking manner the preponderance of venous,
or imperfectly aerated blood throughout the system.

It is not surprising that such impediment to the free circulation of blood through the right side of the heart should
be accompanied by serous infiltration of the serous elements of the blood, or that we should accept the dropsical
infiltration as significant of feebleness and imperfection of the
right heart, arising from exhausting efforts to drive the blood
through the impeded lung structures. But the dropsical
accumulation in these cases of emphysema and chronic
bronchitis signifies something more. Why does the heart
become weak,—attenuated? Why is its cavity increased,
and its walls enfeebled? It is simple enough to point to
the emphysematous lung, with the imperfect process of respiration causing venous blood to accumulate in the pulmonary artery, and to show how the right heart must labour
and become enfeebled by this continuous strain. But why
does the heart become feeble and attenuated? It is a
law governing muscular structures that their nutrition and
development are proportioned to their activity. Rest atte-
nuates the ordinary muscles of volition, activity increases
their power and energy.

In some cases of mitral disease the left heart is embarrassed, and its activity increased; its walls augment in
thickness and contractile power; and the result is an hypertrophied heart, with a contractile energy greater than is
needed; a sledge-hammer kind of impulse, and its blood
driven with unnecessary intensity through the various organs.
Why should not the right heart become hypertrophied; and
why should not its energies and its nutrition increase with
the demands made upon it? I think the appropriate answer

is not difficult to find, and the microscope enables us to give the reason. All these cases of dilatation of the right side of the heart with resulting dropsy, are dependent on an extensive fatty degeneration of the entire heart—not here and there a few filaments fatty, but every bundle of fibre alike degenerated and decayed.

Co-existent with, and perhaps as a cause of the pulmonary disturbance (defect), there is, probably, going on simultaneously in both lung and heart the same process of defective cell development. I have never examined a heart in a case of cardiac dropsy with emphysema in which this fatty degeneration of the muscular fibre of the right heart did not exist to an exaggerated extent. (See Plate V, fig. 6, and Plate VI, fig. 6), where the extreme degree of fatty degeneration of heart fibre in both ventricles and auricles is represented.

I think we may now more clearly comprehend why, in these instances of mechanical impediment to the flow of blood through the lung, the heart, in the place of becoming for a time at least hypertrophied and thickened, it becomes dilated, attenuated, and feeble. Why the heart, instead of compensating by a more powerful contractile and driving power, and overcoming the impediments in the lungs, itself becomes more feeble, and yields slowly but surely to the dilating force of a venous accumulation. Its nutrition fails, and its walls are degenerating in the direction which seems to constitute an inherent law of the organism.

Cardiac dropsy, then, is invariably significant of failing and defective nutrition in the parietes of the heart; and in typical and strongly marked cases is accompanied by an

exaggeration, as it were, of fatty degeneration, in the form of
atheromatous, or opaque patches in the endocardium, even on
the tricuspid valve, with large accumulation of oily-looking
globules, which are mixed up with the characteristic crystal-
line plates of cholesterine.

This condition may be most extensively traced in the
inner membrane of the aorta; in the vascular layer of the
small bronchial tubes; in the fibro-serous sac of the pulmonary cell; in the hepatic cells, and almost in every important
tissue of the body. (See Plates V and VI.)

I had occasion to remark, when speaking of disease of
the mitral valve, that so long as the nutrition of the body
continued good, so long was cell-growth healthy; and whatever changes might be going on in the walls of the left
cavity, they would be in the direction of augmented muscular structure, an hypertrophy of the walls, and an increased
power of the heart's systole. So in relation to the right
ventricle, if the nutrition of the body continued good, we
should expect that healthy cell development would in like
manner continue here also, and increased power of the right
heart follow. But we have seen that the lung defect is
essentially due to a fatty degeneration of tissue. The organism has thus early indicated that the decaying process
has already commenced, and, probably, step by step with
the degeneration of pulmonary tissue there goes on an equal,
co-existing decay of the muscular elements of the heart.
A heart thus failing in the essentials of its nutrition must
eventually become feeble and attenuated, and hence cardiac
dropsy signifies, not so much a mechanical imperfection
interfering with the circulating current, as a debilitated and
ill-nourished organ, becoming feebler and feebler in its con-

tractile power, and eventually unequal to transmit its contents, or carry on the circulation.

Here therefore, as in renal dropsy, we recognise not a local, but a general disorder; a deterioration of cell development not confined to one texture or organ, but wide-spread, and signifying to us in studying the pathology of these disorders, that it is not to the organ which gives the most prominent indication of disturbance that our examination should be limited; but, if we are to render available the results of our observations for the purpose of treatment, we must take into consideration the evidence that has been here offered, that in these dropsical diseases we have a decaying vitality—a decreasing power of elaborating, or forming out of the elements of food, cells fitted for, and equal to, the performance of their several functions.

In such an assembly as this, before so many experienced physicians, I feel how entirely misplaced would be any lengthened remarks on the treatment of these forms of dropsy.

Nor—so far as palliative measures are needed—can I add anything, or suggest other remedies than those generally employed among us.

In hospital practice the cases which come under our care are far advanced in the descending scale of decay, and little more than palliative means can be employed.

Still I permit myself to hope that some of the pathological facts I have submitted for your consideration may deserve a few moments' reflection, and may lead practical men—with reference to the fundamental principles of treatment—to the same conclusions as myself.

In reference, then, to the subject of treatment I will, with

6

your permission, sir, shortly refer to the leading principles
which should govern our advice in all those cases in which the
early elements of disturbance, either cardiac or pulmonary,
may eventually lead to dropsy. I do this rather for the
benefit of my younger hearers than for the edification of
those more immediately before me.

It may appear too much of a truism to say that the leading feature is, by every means, to maintain the nutrition of
the body in the state of the highest efficiency.

But I lay a peculiar emphasis on this apparent truism, to
caution young practitioners against falling into the errors
of common routine practice which makes blistering, and
purging, and other lowering means, the invariable refuge of
the inexperienced.

I can recall to memory the persons of several young people
now grown up to manhood, whose damaged hearts and delicate health, the result of rheumatic inflammation, with the
accompanying shortness of breath, and inability to take any
part in the exciting exercises of youth, become naturally the
source of deep anxiety to their parents.

In these cases all my anxiety was to place the young
patients in the most favorable condition of nourishment.
For a time forbidding all bodily or physical exertion, the
heart was left to the influence of quietude alone; steel and
animal diet were alone prescribed.

In a few months a manifest improvement generally shows
itself. The pallor of the face is exchanged for a more
healthy aspect; the eye regains its natural expression; the
bodily vigour improves; and, in a moderate time, the youthful
instincts of activity and exercise replace the sense of languor
and indifference, which formerly existed. Care is needed

now to limit the amount of exercise, or rather to prevent it taking the form of those efforts in which youth delights, when the heart's powers are momentarily put to greater strain. With such precautions continued up to, and sometimes beyond puberty, the general health being maintained, and no strain being put on the physical powers, the patient in the middle and upper classes of life attains, not perhaps the average duration of life, but at any rate reaches the middle, and, in many cases, even beyond that period, in the fair enjoyment of but little less than falls to the lot of the more vigorous and healthy.

I will briefly refer to the other form—that in which the heart becomes implicated chiefly through the pulmonary disorder.

The leading, the earliest, the most manifest symptom is the cough and expectoration. Pathologically, I would say, the most instructive and suggestive symptom is the expectoration.

Consider that in health no cells are thrown off from the bronchial mucous membrane. A protective layer of ciliated epithelium stretches from the larynx to the entrance of the pulmonary cell. But in chronic bronchitis, and emphysema, a glance at the amount of expectoration in twenty-four hours (bearing in mind that this expectoration is composed altogether of cells and the débris of cells derived from this large extent of surface) will convince us of the exhausting and depressing process which is continuously advancing.

If from the copious expectorated matters in emphysema and bronchorrhœa we take up on the point of a needle a morsel of this muco-purulent expectoration, so small as to

be scarcely visible to the naked eye, the microscope reveals
to us myriads of cells of which the mucus- and pus-cells pre-
dominate: let us reflect for a moment that half a pint, or
even more, of this débris of effete cells is thrown off from
the bronchial membranes in a few hours, and then ask
ourselves to estimate the expenditure of formative power
required to produce this mass of excreta.

A surgeon, when he has to deal with a suppurating surface, relies mainly on nutrition and support. The material
excreted in chronic bronchitis differs only from the purulent
outpouring of a suppurating surface, in that its cellular
elements are more varied, and are not developed at the
expense of the interstitial subjacent tissue. But so far as
the throwing off of these transitional forms of epithelial
cells, the demand made on the vital energies is equal to that
called for by a suppurating surface; and, in my opinion,
needs a not less careful attention to the sustentation of the
powers of the individual.

Old theories still haunt our practice, and an aggravation
of cough and expectoration is still regarded by many as
the signal of that imaginary entity, inflammation; instead
of this, increase in the gravity of the symptoms in reality
signifies a harassed and labouring circulation, a defective
nutrition, and an exhausting development of ill matured cells.

In every case of emphysema and chronic bronchitis, long
before any cardiac complications are manifested, generous
living, fresh air, moderate exercise, and the disuse of every
remedy that is the least depressing in its influence, constitute
the rules of treatment which the pathological facts I have laid
before the College, in my humble opinion, both encourage
and justify.

But we know, sir, that practically such treatment can rarely be carried out, except by persons in a better sphere of life.

For far otherwise is the fate of those who, in the lower class of life, not only have to earn their bread by their physical powers, but who also, from the very deficiency of those powers, are exposed to defective nourishment, scanty clothing, and perhaps irregular and depraved habits.

In such the progress of degeneration is rapid. The tissues everywhere, as in renal dropsy—slowly in some cases, more rapidly in others—lose their power of selection of nitrogenized material for the development of vigorous cell formation. The structures insidiously, but fatally, descend in the scale of development; and tissues, the cells of which should be distinguished by a nucleus of highly nitrogenized matter, now possess but the power of abstracting hydro-carbonized products, and a fatty and amyloid degradation of cell structure is the all-pervading pathological law—conditions which, as they proceed, give unmistakable evidence of decaying powers, and at length reach a point incommensurate with the continuance of life; and the organism which, in the fulness of its life and vigour, was but the expression of the sum of the life of its individual cells now perishes, and yields up its forces to other laws and other combinations of matter.

My original design was to comprise in these lectures the significance of hepatic dropsy, which would have embraced a description of the pathological complications, which are usually associated with cirrhosis, the most frequent form of liver disease, giving rise to dropsy of the belly. But I find, sir, not only will the time allotted to these lectures preclude my entering upon the subject of hepatic dropsy; but I may

add, that Dr. Budd has so completely exhausted the subject
of this form of liver disease, that whatever I could say
on that subject has been in great measure anticipated by
him.

It only now remains for me to express to you, sir, and the
fellows and gentlemen present at these lectures, my thanks
for the kind attention paid to the subjects I have brought
before the college. I venture to hope that they may be
found to contain material for reflection and further inquiry;
and if others shall be induced to consider the significance
of these forms of dropsy from the same point of view as
myself, I shall be encouraged to feel that the suggestions I
have offered with respect to the fundamental principles of
treating these diseases will be better understood, and more
generally and beneficially adopted.

J. E. ADLARD, PRINTER, BARTHOLOMEW CLOSE.

London, New Burlington Street,
April, 1864.

MESSRS. CHURCHILL & SONS'

Publications,

IN

MEDICINE

AND THE VARIOUS BRANCHES OF

NATURAL SCIENCE.

A CLASSIFIED INDEX
TO
MESSRS. CHURCHILL & SONS' CATALOGUE.

CLASSIFIED INDEX.

MR. F. A. ABEL, F.R.S., & MR. C. L. BLOXAM.
HANDBOOK OF CHEMISTRY: THEORETICAL, PRACTICAL, AND TECHNICAL. Second Edition. 8vo. cloth, 15s.

MR. ACTON, M.R.C.S.
I.
A PRACTICAL TREATISE ON DISEASES OF THE URINARY AND GENERATIVE ORGANS IN BOTH SEXES. Third Edition. 8vo. cloth, £1. 1s. With Plates, £1. 11s. 6d. The Plates alone, limp cloth, 10s. 6d.

II.
THE FUNCTIONS AND DISORDERS OF THE REPRODUCTIVE ORGANS IN CHILDHOOD, YOUTH, ADULT AGE, AND ADVANCED LIFE, considered in their Physiological, Social, and Moral Relations. Third Edition. 8vo. cloth, 10s. 6d.

III.
PROSTITUTION: Considered in its Moral, Social, and Sanitary Bearings, with a View to its Amelioration and Regulation. 8vo. cloth, 10s. 6d.

DR. ADAMS, A.M.
A TREATISE ON RHEUMATIC GOUT; OR, CHRONIC RHEUMATIC ARTHRITIS. 8vo. cloth, with a Quarto Atlas of Plates, 21s.

MR. WILLIAM ADAMS, F.R.C.S.
I.
ON THE REPARATIVE PROCESS IN HUMAN TENDONS AFTER SUBCUTANEOUS DIVISION FOR THE CURE OF DEFORMITIES. With Plates. 8vo. cloth, 6s.

II.
SKETCH OF THE PRINCIPLES AND PRACTICE OF SUBCUTANEOUS SURGERY. 8vo. cloth, 2s. 6d.

DR. WILLIAM ADDISON, F.R.S.
I.
CELL THERAPEUTICS. 8vo. cloth, 4s.

II.
ON HEALTHY AND DISEASED STRUCTURE, AND THE TRUE PRINCIPLES OF TREATMENT FOR THE CURE OF DISEASE, ESPECIALLY CONSUMPTION AND SCROFULA, founded on MICROSCOPICAL ANALYSIS. 8vo. cloth, 12s.

DR. SOMERVILLE SCOTT ALISON, M.D. EDIN., F.R.C.P.
THE PHYSICAL EXAMINATION OF THE CHEST IN PULMONARY CONSUMPTION, AND ITS INTERCURRENT DISEASES. With Engravings. 8vo. cloth, 12s.

THE ANATOMICAL REMEMBRANCER; OR, COMPLETE POCKET ANATOMIST. Fifth Edition, carefully Revised. 32mo. cloth, 3s. 6d.

DR. ANDREW ANDERSON, M.D.
TEN LECTURES INTRODUCTORY TO THE STUDY OF FEVER. Post 8vo. cloth, 5s.

DR. MCCALL ANDERSON, M.D.
I.
PARASITIC AFFECTIONS OF THE SKIN. With Engravings. 8vo. cloth, 5s.

II.
PRACTICAL TREATISE ON ECZEMA. With Engravings. 8vo. cloth, 5s.

DR. ARLIDGE.

ON THE STATE OF LUNACY AND THE LEGAL PROVISION FOR THE INSANE; with Observations on the Construction and Organisation of Asylums. 8vo. cloth, 7s.

DR. ALEXANDER ARMSTRONG, R.N.

OBSERVATIONS ON NAVAL HYGIENE AND SCURVY. More particularly as the latter appeared during a Polar Voyage. 8vo. cloth, 5s.

MR. T. J. ASHTON.
I.

ON THE DISEASES, INJURIES, AND MALFORMATIONS OF THE RECTUM AND ANUS. Fourth Edition. 8vo. cloth, 8s.

II.

PROLAPSUS, FISTULA IN ANO, AND HÆMORRHOIDAL AFFECTIONS; their Pathology and Treatment. Second Edition. Post 8vo. cloth, 2s. 6d.

MR. THOS. J. AUSTIN, M.R.C.S. ENG.

A PRACTICAL ACCOUNT OF GENERAL PARALYSIS: Its Mental and Physical Symptoms, Statistics, Causes, Seat, and Treatment. 8vo. cloth, 6s.

DR. THOMAS BALLARD, M.D.

A NEW AND RATIONAL EXPLANATION OF THE DISEASES PECULIAR TO INFANTS AND MOTHERS; with obvious Suggestions for their Prevention and Cure. Post 8vo. cloth, 4s. 6d.

DR. BARCLAY.

A MANUAL OF MEDICAL DIAGNOSIS. Second Edition. Foolscap 8vo. cloth, 8s. 6d.

DR. W. G. BARKER.

ON THE CLIMATE OF WORTHING: its Remedial Influence in Disease, especially of the Lungs. Crown 8vo. cloth, 3s.

DR. BARLOW.

A MANUAL OF THE PRACTICE OF MEDICINE. Second Edition. Fcap. 8vo. cloth, 12s. 6d.

DR. BARNES.

THE PHYSIOLOGY AND TREATMENT OF PLACENTA PRÆVIA; being the Lettsomian Lectures on Midwifery for 1857. Post 8vo. cloth, 6s.

MR. BARWELL, F.R.C.S.
I.

A TREATISE ON DISEASES OF THE JOINTS. With Engravings. 8vo. cloth, 12s.

II.

ON THE CURE OF CLUBFOOT WITHOUT CUTTING TENDONS, and on certain new Methods of Treating other Deformities. With Engravings. Fcap. 8vo. cloth, 3s. 6d.

DR. BASCOME.

A HISTORY OF EPIDEMIC PESTILENCES, FROM THE EARLIEST AGES. 8vo. cloth, 8s.

DR. BASHAM.

ON DROPSY, CONNECTED WITH DISEASE OF THE
KIDNEYS (MORBUS BRIGHTII), and on some other Diseases of those Organs,
associated with Albuminous and Purulent Urine. Illustrated by numerous Drawings
from the Microscope. Second Edition. 8vo. cloth, 9s.

MR. H. F. BAXTER, M.R.C.S.L.

ON ORGANIC POLARITY; showing a Connexion to exist between
Organic Forces and Ordinary Polar Forces. Crown 8vo. cloth, 5s.

MR. BATEMAN.

MAGNACOPIA: A Practical Library of Profitable Knowledge, commu-
nicating the general Minutiæ of Chemical and Pharmaceutic Routine, together with the
generality of Secret Forms of Preparations. Third Edition. 18mo. 6s.

MR. LIONEL J. BEALE, M.R.C.S.

I.

THE LAWS OF HEALTH IN THEIR RELATIONS TO MIND
AND BODY. A Series of Letters from an Old Practitioner to a Patient. Post 8vo.
cloth, 7s. 6d.

II.

HEALTH AND DISEASE, IN CONNECTION WITH THE
GENERAL PRINCIPLES OF HYGIENE. Fcap. 8vo., 2s. 6d.

DR. BEALE, F.R.S.

I.

URINE, URINARY DEPOSITS, AND CALCULI: and on the
Treatment of Urinary Diseases. Numerous Engravings. Second Edition, much Enlarged.
Post 8vo. cloth, 8s. 6d.

II.

HOW TO WORK WITH THE MICROSCOPE. Illustrated Edition.
Crown 8vo. cloth, 5s. 6d.

III.

THE MICROSCOPE, IN ITS APPLICATION TO PRACTICAL
MEDICINE. With a Coloured Plate, and 270 Woodcuts. Second Edition. 8vo.
cloth, 14s.

IV.

ILLUSTRATIONS OF THE SALTS OF URINE, URINARY
DEPOSITS, and CALCULI. 37 Plates, containing upwards of 170 Figures copied
from Nature, with descriptive Letterpress. 8vo. cloth, 9s. 6d.

MR. BEASLEY.

I.

THE BOOK OF PRESCRIPTIONS; containing 3000 Prescriptions.
Collected from the Practice of the most eminent Physicians and Surgeons, English
and Foreign. Second Edition. 18mo. cloth, 6s.

II.

THE DRUGGIST'S GENERAL RECEIPT-BOOK; comprising a
copious Veterinary Formulary and Table of Veterinary Materia Medica; Patent and
Proprietary Medicines, Druggists' Nostrums, &c.; Perfumery, Skin Cosmetics, Hair
Cosmetics, and Teeth Cosmetics; Beverages, Dietetic Articles, and Condiments; Trade
Chemicals, Miscellaneous Preparations and Compounds used in the Arts, &c.; with
useful Memoranda and Tables. Fifth Edition. 18mo. cloth, 6s.

III.

THE POCKET FORMULARY AND SYNOPSIS OF THE
BRITISH AND FOREIGN PHARMACOPŒIAS; comprising standard and
approved Formulæ for the Preparations and Compounds employed in Medical Practice.
Seventh Edition, corrected and enlarged. 18mo. cloth, 6s.

DR. HENRY BENNET.

I.

A PRACTICAL TREATISE ON INFLAMMATION AND OTHER DISEASES OF THE UTERUS. Fourth Edition, revised, with Additions. 8vo. cloth, 16s.

II.

A REVIEW OF THE PRESENT STATE OF UTERINE PATHOLOGY. 8vo. cloth, 4s.

III.

NUTRITION IN HEALTH AND DISEASE. Post 8vo. cloth, 5s.

IV.

MENTONE, THE RIVIERA, CORSICA, AND BIARRITZ, AS WINTER CLIMATES. Second Edition. Post 8vo. cloth, 5s.

PROFESSOR BENTLEY, F.L.S.

A MANUAL OF BOTANY. With nearly 1,200 Engravings on Wood. Fcap. 8vo. cloth, 12s. 6d.

MR. HENRY HEATHER BIGG.

I.

THE MECHANICAL APPLIANCES NECESSARY FOR THE TREATMENT OF DEFORMITIES.
PART I.—The Lower Limbs. Post 8vo. cloth, 4s.
PART II.—The Spine and Upper Extremities. Post 8vo. cloth, 4s. 6d.

II.

ARTIFICIAL LIMBS; THEIR CONSTRUCTION AND APPLICATION. With Engravings on Wood. 8vo. cloth, 3s.

DR. BILLING, F.R.S.

ON DISEASES OF THE LUNGS AND HEART. 8vo. cloth, 6s.

DR. S. B. BIRCH, M.D.

CONSTIPATED BOWELS: the Various Causes and the Rational Means of Cure. Second Edition. Post 8vo. cloth, 3s. 6d.

DR. GOLDING BIRD, F.R.S.

I.

URINARY DEPOSITS; THEIR DIAGNOSIS, PATHOLOGY, AND THERAPEUTICAL INDICATIONS. With Engravings. Fifth Edition. Edited by E. LLOYD BIRKETT, M.D. Post 8vo. cloth, 10s. 6d.

II.

ELEMENTS OF NATURAL PHILOSOPHY; being an Experimental Introduction to the Study of the Physical Sciences. With numerous Engravings. Fifth Edition. Edited by CHARLES BROOKE, M.B. Cantab., F.R.S. Fcap. 8vo. cloth, 12s. 6d.

MR. BISHOP, F.R.S.

I.

ON DEFORMITIES OF THE HUMAN BODY, their Pathology and Treatment. With Engravings on Wood. 8vo. cloth, 10s.

II.

ON ARTICULATE SOUNDS, AND ON THE CAUSES AND CURE OF IMPEDIMENTS OF SPEECH. 8vo. cloth, 4s.

MR. P. HINCKES BIRD, F.R.C.S.

PRACTICAL TREATISE ON THE DISEASES OF CHILDREN
AND INFANTS AT THE BREAST. Translated from the French of M. Bouchut,
with Notes and Additions. 8vo. cloth. 20s.

MR. ROBERT HOWARTH BLAKE, M.R.C.S.L.

ON DISEASES OF THE SKIN IN CHILDREN. From the French
of CAILLAULT. Re-issued, much enlarged. Post 8vo. cloth, 8s. 6d.

DR. BLAKISTON, F.R.S.

PRACTICAL OBSERVATIONS ON CERTAIN DISEASES OF
THE CHEST; and on the Principles of Auscultation. 8vo. cloth, 12s.

MR. JOHN E. BOWMAN, & MR. C. L. BLOXAM.

I.

PRACTICAL CHEMISTRY, including Analysis. With numerous Illustrations on Wood. Fourth Edition. Foolscap 8vo. cloth, 6s. 6d.

II.

MEDICAL CHEMISTRY; with Illustrations on Wood. Fourth Edition,
carefully revised. Fcap. 8vo. cloth, 6s. 6d.

DR. JAMES BRIGHT.

ON DISEASES OF THE HEART, LUNGS, & AIR PASSAGES;
with a Review of the several Climates recommended in these Affections. Third Edition. Post 8vo. cloth, 9s.

DR. BRINTON.

I.

THE DISEASES OF THE STOMACH, with an Introduction on its
Anatomy and Physiology; being Lectures delivered at St. Thomas's Hospital. Post 8vo.
cloth, 10s. 6d.

II.

THE SYMPTOMS, PATHOLOGY, AND TREATMENT OF
ULCER OF THE STOMACH. Post 8vo. cloth, 5s.

MR. BERNARD E. BRODHURST, F.R.C.S.

I.

ON LATERAL CURVATURE OF THE SPINE: its Pathology and
Treatment. Post 8vo. cloth, with Plates, 3s.

II.

ON THE NATURE AND TREATMENT OF CLUBFOOT AND
ANALOGOUS DISTORTIONS involving the TIBIO-TARSAL ARTICULATION.
With Engravings on Wood. 8vo. cloth, 4s. 6d.

III.

PRACTICAL OBSERVATIONS ON THE DISEASES OF THE
JOINTS INVOLVING ANCHYLOSIS, and on the TREATMENT for the
RESTORATION of MOTION. Third Edition, much enlarged, 8vo. cloth, 4s. 6d.

MR. THOMAS BRYANT, F.R.C.S.

I.

ON THE DISEASES AND INJURIES OF THE JOINTS
CLINICAL AND PATHOLOGICAL OBSERVATIONS. Post 8vo. cloth, 7s. 6d

II.

THE SURGICAL DISEASES OF CHILDREN. The Lettsomian
Lectures, delivered March, 1863. Post 8vo. cloth, 5s.

DR. BRYCE.

ENGLAND AND FRANCE BEFORE SEBASTOPOL, looked at from a Medical Point of View. 8vo. cloth, 6s.

DR. BUDD, F.R.S.

I.

ON DISEASES OF THE LIVER.

Illustrated with Coloured Plates and Engravings on Wood. Third Edition. 8vo. cloth, 16s.

II.

ON THE ORGANIC DISEASES AND FUNCTIONAL DIS-ORDERS OF THE STOMACH. 8vo. cloth, 9s.

DR. JOHN CHARLES BUCKNILL, & DR. DANIEL H. TUKE.

A MANUAL OF PSYCHOLOGICAL MEDICINE: containing the History, Nosology, Description, Statistics, Diagnosis, Pathology, and Treatment of Insanity. Second Edition. 8vo. cloth, 15s.

MR. CALLENDER, F.R.C.S.

FEMORAL RUPTURE: Anatomy of the Parts concerned. With Plates. 8vo. cloth, 4s.

DR. JOHN M. CAMPLIN, F.L.S.

ON DIABETES, AND ITS SUCCESSFUL TREATMENT. Third Edition, by Dr. Glover. Fcap. 8vo. cloth, 3s. 6d.

MR. ROBERT B. CARTER, M.R.C.S.

I.

ON THE INFLUENCE OF EDUCATION AND TRAINING IN PREVENTING DISEASES OF THE NERVOUS SYSTEM. Fcap. 8vo., 6s.

II.

THE PATHOLOGY AND TREATMENT OF HYSTERIA. Post 8vo. cloth, 4s. 6d.

DR. CARPENTER, F.R.S.

I.

PRINCIPLES OF HUMAN PHYSIOLOGY. With numerous Illustrations on Steel and Wood. Fifth Edition. 8vo. cloth, 26s.

II.

PRINCIPLES OF COMPARATIVE PHYSIOLOGY. Illustrated with 300 Engravings on Wood. Fourth Edition. 8vo. cloth, 24s.

III.

A MANUAL OF PHYSIOLOGY. With numerous Illustrations on Steel and Wood. Third Edition. Fcap. 8vo. cloth, 12s. 6d.

IV.

THE MICROSCOPE AND ITS REVELATIONS. With numerous Engravings on Steel and Wood. Third Edition. Fcap. 8vo. cloth, 12s. 6d.

DR. CHAMBERS.

I.

THE RENEWAL OF LIFE. Clinical Lectures illustrative of a Restorative System of Medicine. Second Edition. Post 8vo. cloth, 6s. 6d.

II.

DIGESTION AND ITS DERANGEMENTS. Post 8vo. cloth, 10s. 6d.

DR. CHANCE, M.B.

VIRCHOW'S CELLULAR PATHOLOGY, AS BASED UPON PHYSIOLOGICAL AND PATHOLOGICAL HISTOLOGY. With 144 Engravings on Wood. 8vo. cloth, 16s.

MR. H. T. CHAPMAN, F.R.C.S.

I.

THE TREATMENT OF OBSTINATE ULCERS AND CUTANEOUS ERUPTIONS OF THE LEG WITHOUT CONFINEMENT. Third Edition. Post 8vo. cloth, 3s. 6d.

II.

VARICOSE VEINS: their Nature, Consequences, and Treatment, Palliative and Curative. Post 8vo. cloth, 3s. 6d.

MR. PYE HENRY CHAVASSE, F.R.C.S.

I.

ADVICE TO A MOTHER ON THE MANAGEMENT OF HER OFFSPRING. Seventh Edition. Foolscap 8vo., 2s. 6d.

II.

ADVICE TO A WIFE ON THE MANAGEMENT OF HER OWN HEALTH. With an Introductory Chapter, especially addressed to a Young Wife. Fifth Edition. Fcap. 8vo., 2s. 6d.

MR. LE GROS CLARK, F.R.C.S.

OUTLINES OF SURGERY; being an Epitome of the Lectures on the Principles and the Practice of Surgery, delivered at St. Thomas's Hospital. Fcap. 8vo. cloth, 5s.

MR. JOHN CLAY, M.R.C.S.

KIWISCH ON DISEASES OF THE OVARIES: Translated, by permission, from the last German Edition of his Clinical Lectures on the Special Pathology and Treatment of the Diseases of Women. With Notes, and an Appendix on the Operation of Ovariotomy. Royal 12mo. cloth, 16s.

DR. CONOLLY.

THE CONSTRUCTION AND GOVERNMENT OF LUNATIC ASYLUMS AND HOSPITALS FOR THE INSANE. With Plans. Post 8vo. cloth, 6s.

MR. COOLEY.

COMPREHENSIVE SUPPLEMENT TO THE PHARMACOPŒIAS.

THE CYCLOPÆDIA OF PRACTICAL RECEIPTS, AND COLLATERAL INFORMATION IN THE ARTS, PROFESSIONS, MANUFACTURES, AND TRADES, INCLUDING MEDICINE, PHARMACY, AND DOMESTIC ECONOMY; designed as a Compendious Book of Reference for the Manufacturer, Tradesman, Amateur, and Heads of Families. Third and greatly enlarged Edition, 8vo. cloth, 26s.

SIR ASTLEY COOPER, BART., F.R.S.

ON THE STRUCTURE AND DISEASES OF THE TESTIS. With 24 Plates. Second Edition. Royal 4to., 20s.

MR. W. WHITE COOPER.

I.

ON WOUNDS AND INJURIES OF THE EYE. Illustrated by 17 Coloured Figures and 41 Woodcuts. 8vo. cloth, 12s.

II.

ON NEAR SIGHT, AGED SIGHT, IMPAIRED VISION, AND THE MEANS OF ASSISTING SIGHT. With 31 Illustrations on Wood. Second Edition. Fcap. 8vo. cloth, 7s. 6d.

MR. COOPER.

A DICTIONARY OF PRACTICAL SURGERY AND ENCYCLO-
PÆDIA OF SURGICAL SCIENCE. New Edition, brought down to the present
time. By SAMUEL A. LANE, F.R.C.S., assisted by various eminent Surgeons. Vol. I.,
8vo. cloth, £1. 5s.

MR. HOLMES COOTE, F.R.C.S.

A REPORT ON SOME IMPORTANT POINTS IN THE
TREATMENT OF SYPHILIS. 8vo. cloth, 5s.

DR. COTTON.
I.

ON CONSUMPTION: Its Nature, Symptoms, and Treatment. To
which Essay was awarded the Fothergillian Gold Medal of the Medical Society of
London. Second Edition. 8vo. cloth, 8s.

II.

PHTHISIS AND THE STETHOSCOPE; OR, THE PHYSICAL
SIGNS OF CONSUMPTION. Third Edition. Foolscap 8vo. cloth, 3s.

MR. COULSON.
I.

ON DISEASES OF THE BLADDER AND PROSTATE GLAND.
The Fifth Edition, revised and enlarged. 8vo. cloth, 10s. 6d.

II.

ON LITHOTRITY AND LITHOTOMY; with Engravings on Wood.
8vo. cloth, 8s.

MR. WILLIAM CRAIG, L.F.P.S., GLASGOW.

ON THE INFLUENCE OF VARIATIONS OF ELECTRIC
TENSION AS THE REMOTE CAUSE OF EPIDEMIC AND OTHER
DISEASES. 8vo. cloth, 10s.

MR. CURLING, F.R.S.
I.

OBSERVATIONS ON DISEASES OF THE RECTUM. Third
Edition. 8vo. cloth, 7s. 6d.
II.

A PRACTICAL TREATISE ON DISEASES OF THE TESTIS,
SPERMATIC CORD, AND SCROTUM. Second Edition, with Additions. 8vo.
cloth, 14s.

DR. DALRYMPLE, M.R.C.P., F.R.C.S.

THE CLIMATE OF EGYPT: METEOROLOGICAL AND MEDI-
CAL OBSERVATIONS, with Practical Hints for Invalid Travellers. Post 8vo. cloth, 4s.

MR. JOHN DALRYMPLE, F.R.S., F.R.C.S.

PATHOLOGY OF THE HUMAN EYE. Complete in Nine Fasciculi:
imperial 4to., 20s. each; half-bound morocco, gilt tops, 9l. 15s.

DR. DAVEY
I.

THE GANGLIONIC NERVOUS SYSTEM: its Structure, Functions,
and Diseases. 8vo. cloth, 9s.
II.

ON THE NATURE AND PROXIMATE CAUSE OF IN-
SANITY. Post 8vo. cloth, 3s.

DR. HERBERT DAVIES.

ON THE PHYSICAL DIAGNOSIS OF DISEASES OF THE LUNGS AND HEART. Second Edition. Post 8vo. cloth, 8s.

DR. HALL DAVIS.

ILLUSTRATIONS OF DIFFICULT PARTURITION. Post 8vo. cloth, 6s. 6d.

MR. DIXON.

A GUIDE TO THE PRACTICAL STUDY OF DISEASES OF THE EYE. Second Edition. Post 8vo. cloth, 9s.

DR. DOBELL.

I.

DEMONSTRATIONS OF DISEASES IN THE CHEST, AND THEIR PHYSICAL DIAGNOSIS. With Coloured Plates. 8vo. cloth, 12s. 6d.

II.

LECTURES ON THE GERMS AND VESTIGES OF DISEASE, and on the Prevention of the Invasion and Fatality of Disease by Periodical Examinations. 8vo. cloth, 6s. 6d.

III.

A MANUAL OF DIET AND REGIMEN FOR PHYSICIAN AND PATIENT. Crown 8vo. cloth, 1s. 6d.

DR. TOOGOOD DOWNING.

NEURALGIA: its various Forms, Pathology, and Treatment. THE JACKSONIAN PRIZE ESSAY FOR 1850. 8vo. cloth, 10s. 6d.

DR. DRUITT, F.R.C.S.

THE SURGEON'S VADE-MECUM; with numerous Engravings on Wood. Eighth Edition. Foolscap 8vo. cloth, 12s. 6d.

MR. DUNN, F.R.C.S.

AN ESSAY ON PHYSIOLOGICAL PSYCHOLOGY. 8vo. cloth, 4s.

SIR JAMES EYRE, M.D.

I.

THE STOMACH AND ITS DIFFICULTIES. Fifth Edition. Fcap. 8vo. cloth, 2s. 6d.

II.

PRACTICAL REMARKS ON SOME EXHAUSTING DIS-EASES. Second Edition. Post 8vo. cloth, 4s. 6d.

DR. FENWICK.

ON SCROFULA AND CONSUMPTION. Clergyman's Sore Throat, Catarrh, Croup, Bronchitis, Asthma. Fcap. 8vo., 2s. 6d.

MR. FERGUSSON, F.R.S.

A SYSTEM OF PRACTICAL SURGERY; with numerous Illustrations on Wood. Fourth Edition. Fcap. 8vo. cloth, 12s. 6d.

MR. FLOWER, F.R.C.S.

DIAGRAMS OF THE NERVES OF THE HUMAN BODY, exhibiting their Origin, Divisions, and Connexions, with their Distribution to the various Regions of the Cutaneous Surface, and to all the Muscles. Folio, containing Six Plates, 14s.

SIR JOHN FORBES, M.D., D.C.L. (OXON.), F.R.S.

NATURE AND ART IN THE CURE OF DISEASE. Second Edition. Post 8vo. cloth, 6s.

MR. FOWNES, PH.D., F.R.S.

I.

A MANUAL OF CHEMISTRY; with 187 Illustrations on Wood. Ninth Edition. Fcap. 8vo. cloth, 12s. 6d.
Edited by H. BENCE JONES, M.D., F.R.S., and A. W. HOFMANN, PH.D., F.R.S.

II.

CHEMISTRY, AS EXEMPLIFYING THE WISDOM AND BENEFICENCE OF GOD. Second Edition. Fcap. 8vo. cloth, 4s. 6d.

III.

INTRODUCTION TO QUALITATIVE ANALYSIS. Post 8vo. cloth, 2s.

DR. D. J. T. FRANCIS.

CHANGE OF CLIMATE; considered as a Remedy in Dyspeptic, Pulmonary, and other Chronic Affections; with an Account of the most Eligible Places of Residence for Invalids, at different Seasons of the Year; and an Appendix on the Mineral Springs of the Pyrenees, Vichy, and Aix les Bains. Post 8vo. cloth, 8s. 6d.

MR. J. G. FRENCH, F.R.C.S.

THE NATURE OF CHOLERA INVESTIGATED. Second Edition. 8vo. cloth, 4s.

C. REMIGIUS FRESENIUS.

A SYSTEM OF INSTRUCTION IN CHEMICAL ANALYSIS, Edited by LLOYD BULLOCK, F.C.S.
QUALITATIVE. Sixth Edition, with Coloured Plate illustrating Spectrum Analysis. 8vo. cloth, 10s. 6d.——QUANTITATIVE. Third Edition. 8vo. cloth, 16s.

DR. FULLER.

I.

ON DISEASES OF THE CHEST, including Diseases of the Heart and Great Vessels. With Engravings. 8vo. cloth, 12s. 6d.

II.

ON DISEASES OF THE HEART AND GREAT VESSELS. 8vo. cloth, 7s. 6d.

III.

ON RHEUMATISM, RHEUMATIC GOUT, AND SCIATICA: their Pathology, Symptoms, and Treatment. Third Edition. 8vo. cloth, 12s. 6d.

DR. GAIRDNER.

ON GOUT; its History, its Causes, and its Cure. Fourth Edition. Post 8vo. cloth, 8s. 6d.

MR. GALLOWAY.

I.

THE FIRST STEP IN CHEMISTRY. Third Edition. Fcap. 8vo. cloth, 5s.

II.

THE SECOND STEP IN CHEMISTRY; or, the Student's Guide to the Higher Branches of the Science. With Engravings. 8vo. cloth, 10s.

III.

A MANUAL OF QUALITATIVE ANALYSIS. Third Edition. Post 8vo. cloth, 5s.

IV.

CHEMICAL TABLES. On Five Large Sheets, for School and Lecture Rooms. Second Edition. 4s. 6d.

MR. F. J. GANT, F.R.C.S.

I.

THE PRINCIPLES OF SURGERY: Clinical, Medical, and Operative. With Engravings. 8vo. cloth, 18s.

II.

THE IRRITABLE BLADDER: its Causes and Curative Treatment. Post 8vo. cloth, 4s 6d.

DR. GIBB, M.R.C.P.

ON DISEASES OF THE THROAT AND WINDPIPE, as reflected by the Laryngoscope. Second Edition. With 116 Engravings. Post 8vo. cloth, 10s. 6d.

MRS. GODFREY.

ON THE NATURE, PREVENTION, TREATMENT, AND CURE OF SPINAL CURVATURES and DEFORMITIES of the CHEST and LIMBS, without ARTIFICIAL SUPPORTS or any MECHANICAL APPLIANCES. Third Edition, Revised and Enlarged. 8vo. cloth, 5s.

DR. GORDON, M.D., C.B.

CHINA, FROM A MEDICAL POINT OF VIEW, IN 1860 AND 1861; With a Chapter on Nagasaki as a Sanatarium. With Plans. 8vo. cloth, 10s. 6d.

DR. GRANVILLE, F.R.S.

I.

THE MINERAL SPRINGS OF VICHY: their Efficacy in the Treatment of Gout, Indigestion, Gravel, &c. 8vo. cloth, 5s.

II.

ON SUDDEN DEATH. Post 8vo., 2s. 6d.

DR. GRAVES, M.D., F.R.S.

STUDIES IN PHYSIOLOGY AND MEDICINE. Edited by Dr. Stokes. With Portrait and Memoir. 8vo. cloth, 14s.

MR. GRIFFITHS.

CHEMISTRY OF THE FOUR SEASONS— Spring, Summer, Autumn, Winter. Illustrated with Engravings on Wood. Second Edition. Foolscap 8vo. cloth, 7s. 6d.

DR. GULLY.

THE SIMPLE TREATMENT OF DISEASE; deduced from the Methods of Expectancy and Revulsion. 18mo. cloth, 4s.

DR. GUY.

HOOPER'S PHYSICIAN'S VADE-MECUM; OR, MANUAL OF THE PRINCIPLES AND PRACTICE OF PHYSIC. New Edition, considerably enlarged, and rewritten. Foolscap 8vo. cloth, 12s. 6d.

GUY'S HOSPITAL REPORTS. Third Series. Vols. I. to IX., 8vo., 7s. 6d. each.

DR. HABERSHON, F.R.C.P.

I.

PATHOLOGICAL AND PRACTICAL OBSERVATIONS ON DISEASES OF THE ABDOMEN, comprising those of the Stomach and other Parts of the Alimentary Canal, Œsophagus, Stomach, Cæcum, Intestines, and Peritoneum. Second Edition, with Plates. 8vo. cloth, 14s.

II.

ON THE INJURIOUS EFFECTS OF MERCURY IN THE TREATMENT OF DISEASE. Post 8vo. cloth, 3s. 6d.

DR. C. RADCLYFFE HALL.

TORQUAY IN ITS MEDICAL ASPECT AS A RESORT FOR PULMONARY INVALIDS. Post 8vo. cloth, 5s.

DR. MARSHALL HALL, F.R.S.

I.

PRONE AND POSTURAL RESPIRATION IN DROWNING AND OTHER FORMS OF APNŒA OR SUSPENDED RESPIRATION. Post 8vo. cloth. 5s.

II.

PRACTICAL OBSERVATIONS AND SUGGESTIONS IN MEDICINE. Second Series. Post 8vo. cloth, 8s. 6d.

MR. HARDWICH.

A MANUAL OF PHOTOGRAPHIC CHEMISTRY. Seventh Edition. Foolscap 8vo. cloth, 7s. 6d.

MR. HARE, F.R.C.S.

PRACTICAL OBSERVATIONS ON THE PREVENTION, CAUSES, AND TREATMENT OF CURVATURES OF THE SPINE; with Engravings. Third Edition. 8vo. cloth, 6s.

DR. J. BOWER HARRISON, M.D., M.R.C.P.

I.

LETTERS TO A YOUNG PRACTITIONER ON THE DISEASES OF CHILDREN. Foolscap 8vo. cloth, 3s.

II.

ON THE CONTAMINATION OF WATER BY THE POISON OF LEAD, and its Effects on the Human Body. Foolscap 8vo. cloth, 3s. 6d.

DR. HARTWIG.

I.

ON SEA BATHING AND SEA AIR. Second Edition. Fcap. 8vo., 2s. 6d.

II.

ON THE PHYSICAL EDUCATION OF CHILDREN. Fcap. 8vo., 2s. 6d.

DR. A. H. HASSALL.

I.

THE URINE, IN HEALTH AND DISEASE; being an Explanation of the Composition of the Urine, and of the Pathology and Treatment of Urinary and Renal Disorders. Second Edition. With 79 Engravings (23 Coloured). Post 8vo. cloth, 12s. 6d.

II.

THE MICROSCOPIC ANATOMY OF THE HUMAN BODY, IN HEALTH AND DISEASE. Illustrated with Several Hundred Drawings in Colour. Two vols. 8vo. cloth, £1. 10s.

MR. ALFRED HAVILAND, M.R.C.S.

CLIMATE, WEATHER, AND DISEASE; being a Sketch of the Opinions of the most celebrated Ancient and Modern Writers with regard to the Influence of Climate and Weather in producing Disease. With Four coloured Engravings. 8vo. cloth, 7s.

DR. HEADLAND.

ON THE ACTION OF MEDICINES IN THE SYSTEM. Being the Prize Essay to which the Medical Society of London awarded the Fothergillian Gold Medal for 1852. Third Edition. 8vo. cloth, 12s. 6d.

DR. HEALE.
I.

A TREATISE ON THE PHYSIOLOGICAL ANATOMY OF THE LUNGS. With Engravings. 8vo. cloth, 8s.

II.

A TREATISE ON VITAL CAUSES. 8vo. cloth, 9s.

MR. CHRISTOPHER HEATH, F.R.C.S.

A MANUAL OF MINOR SURGERY AND BANDAGING, FOR THE USE OF HOUSE-SURGEONS, DRESSERS, AND JUNIOR PRAC-TITIONERS. With Illustrations. Second Edition. Fcap. 8vo. cloth, 5s.

MR. HIGGINBOTTOM, F.R.S., F.R.C.S.E.

ON THE NITRATE OF SILVER: WITH FULL DIRECTIONS FOR ITS APPLICATION IN THE TREATMENT OF INFLAMMATION, WOUNDS, AND ULCERS. Part I., Second Edition, 5s.; Part II., 2s. 6d.

DR. HINDS.

THE HARMONIES OF PHYSICAL SCIENCE IN RELATION TO THE HIGHER SENTIMENTS; with Observations on Medical Studies, and on the Moral and Scientific Relations of Medical Life. Post 8vo. cloth, 4s.

MR. J. A. HINGESTON, M.R.C.S.

TOPICS OF THE DAY, MEDICAL, SOCIAL, AND SCIENTIFIC. Crown 8vo. cloth, 7s. 6d.

DR. HODGES.

THE NATURE, PATHOLOGY, AND TREATMENT OF PUER-PERAL CONVULSIONS. Crown 8vo. cloth, 3s.

DR. DECIMUS HODGSON.

THE PROSTATE GLAND, AND ITS ENLARGEMENT IN OLD AGE. With 12 Plates. Royal 8vo. cloth, 6s.

MR. JABEZ HOGG.

A MANUAL OF OPHTHALMOSCOPIC SURGERY; being a Practical Treatise on the Use of the Ophthalmoscope in Diseases of the Eye. Third Edition. With Coloured Plates. 8vo. cloth, 10s. 6d.

MR. LUTHER HOLDEN, F.R.C.S.
I.

HUMAN OSTEOLOGY: with Plates, showing the Attachments of the Muscles. Third Edition. 8vo. cloth, 16s.

II.

A MANUAL OF THE DISSECTION OF THE HUMAN BODY. With Engravings on Wood. Second Edition. 8vo. cloth, 16s.

MR. BARNARD HOLT, F.R.C.S.

ON THE IMMEDIATE TREATMENT OF STRICTURE OF THE URETHRA. Second Edition, Enlarged. 8vo. cloth, 3s.

MR. C. HOLTHOUSE.
I.

ON SQUINTING, PARALYTIC AFFECTIONS OF THE EYE, and CERTAIN FORMS OF IMPAIRED VISION. Fcap. 8vo. cloth, 4s. 6d.

II.

LECTURES ON STRABISMUS, delivered at the Westminster Hospital. 8vo. cloth, 4s.

DR. W. CHARLES HOOD.

SUGGESTIONS FOR THE FUTURE PROVISION OF CRIMINAL LUNATICS. 8vo. cloth, 5s. 6d.

DR. P. HOOD.

THE SUCCESSFUL TREATMENT OF SCARLET FEVER; also, OBSERVATIONS ON THE PATHOLOGY AND TREATMENT OF CROWING INSPIRATIONS OF INFANTS. Post 8vo. cloth, 5s.

MR. JOHN HORSLEY.

A CATECHISM OF CHEMICAL PHILOSOPHY; being a Familiar Exposition of the Principles of Chemistry and Physics. With Engravings on Wood. Designed for the Use of Schools and Private Teachers. Post 8vo. cloth, 6s. 6d.

DR. HUFELAND.

THE ART OF PROLONGING LIFE. Second Edition. Edited by ERASMUS WILSON, F.R.S. Foolscap 8vo., 2s. 6d.

MR. W. CURTIS HUGMAN, F.R.C.S.

ON HIP-JOINT DISEASE; with reference especially to Treatment by Mechanical Means for the Relief of Contraction and Deformity of the Affected Limb. 8vo. cloth, 3s. 6d.

MR. HULKE, F.R.C.S.

A PRACTICAL TREATISE ON THE USE OF THE OPHTHALMOSCOPE. Being the Jacksonian Prize Essay for 1859. Royal 8vo. cloth, 8s.

DR. HENRY HUNT.

ON HEARTBURN AND INDIGESTION. 8vo. cloth, 5s.

PROFESSOR HUXLEY, F.R.S.

LECTURES ON THE ELEMENTS OF COMPARATIVE ANATOMY.—ON CLASSIFICATON AND THE SKULL. With 111 Illustrations. 8vo. cloth, 10s. 6d.

MR. JONATHAN HUTCHINSON, F.R.C.S.

A CLINICAL MEMOIR ON CERTAIN DISEASES OF THE EYE AND EAR, CONSEQUENT ON INHERITED SYPHILIS; with an appended Chapter of Commentaries on the Transmission of Syphilis from Parent to Offspring, and its more remote Consequences. With Plates and Woodcuts, 8vo. cloth, 9s.

DR. INMAN, M.R.C.P.

I.

ON MYALGIA: ITS NATURE, CAUSES, AND TREATMENT; being a Treatise on Painful and other Affections of the Muscular System. Second Edition. 8vo. cloth, 9s.

II.

FOUNDATION FOR A NEW THEORY AND PRACTICE OF MEDICINE. Second Edition. Crown 8vo. cloth, 10s.

DR. ARTHUR JACOB, F.R.C.S.

A TREATISE ON THE INFLAMMATIONS OF THE EYE-BALL. Foolscap 8vo. cloth, 5s.

MR. J. H. JAMES, F.R.C.S.

PRACTICAL OBSERVATIONS ON THE OPERATIONS FOR STRANGULATED HERNIA. 8vo. cloth, 5s.

DR. PROSSER JAMES, M.D.

SORE-THROAT: ITS NATURE, VARIETIES, AND TREAT- MENT; including the Use of the LARYNGOSCOPE as an Aid to Diagnosis. Post 8vo. cloth, 4s. 6d.

DR. HANDFIELD JONES, F.R.S., & DR. EDWARD H. SIEVEKING.

A MANUAL OF PATHOLOGICAL ANATOMY. Illustrated with numerous Engravings on Wood. Foolscap 8vo. cloth, 12s. 6d.

DR. JAMES JONES, M.D., M.R.C.P.

ON THE USE OF PERCHLORIDE OF IRON AND OTHER CHALYBEATE SALTS IN THE TREATMENT OF CONSUMPTION. Crown 8vo. cloth, 3s. 6d.

MR. WHARTON JONES, F.R.S.

I.

A MANUAL OF THE PRINCIPLES AND PRACTICE OF OPHTHALMIC MEDICINE AND SURGERY; illustrated with Engravings, plain and coloured. Second Edition. Foolscap 8vo. cloth, 12s. 6d.

II.

THE WISDOM AND BENEFICENCE OF THE ALMIGHTY, AS DISPLAYED IN THE SENSE OF VISION; being the Actonian Prize Essay for 1851. With Illustrations on Steel and Wood. Foolscap 8vo. cloth, 4s. 6d.

III.

DEFECTS OF SIGHT: their Nature, Causes, Prevention, and General Management. Fcap. 8vo. 2s. 6d.

IV.

A CATECHISM OF THE MEDICINE AND SURGERY OF THE EYE AND EAR. For the Clinical Use of Hospital Students. Fcap. 8vo. 2s. 6d.

V.

A CATECHISM OF THE PHYSIOLOGY AND PHILOSOPHY OF BODY, SENSE, AND MIND. For Use in Schools and Colleges. Fcap. 8vo., 2s. 6d.

MR. FURNEAUX JORDAN, M.R.C.S.

AN INTRODUCTION TO CLINICAL SURGERY; WITH A Method of Investigating and Reporting Surgical Cases. Fcap. 8vo. cloth, 5s.

MR. JUDD.

A PRACTICAL TREATISE ON URETHRITIS AND SYPHI- LIS: including Observations on the Power of the Menstruous Fluid, and of the Discharge from Leucorrhœa and Sores to produce Urethritis: with a variety of Examples, Experiments, Remedies, and Cures. 8vo. cloth, £1. 5s.

DR. LAENNEC.

A MANUAL OF AUSCULTATION AND PERCUSSION. Translated and Edited by J. B. SHARPE, M.R.C.S. 3s.

DR. LANE, M.A.

HYDROPATHY; OR, HYGIENIC MEDICINE. An Explanatory Essay. Second Edition. Post 8vo. cloth, 5s.

MR. LAWRENCE, F.R.S.

I.

LECTURES ON SURGERY. 8vo. cloth, 16s.

II.

A TREATISE ON RUPTURES. The Fifth Edition, considerably enlarged. 8vo. cloth, 16s.

MISS LE HARDY.

THE HOME NURSE, AND MANUAL FOR THE SICK ROOM. Foolscap 8vo. cloth, 6s.

DR. LEARED, M.R.C.P.

IMPERFECT DIGESTION: ITS CAUSES AND TREATMENT. Third Edition. Foolscap 8vo. cloth, 4s.

DR. EDWIN LEE.

I.

THE EFFECT OF CLIMATE ON TUBERCULOUS DISEASE, with Notices of the chief Foreign Places of Winter Resort. Small 8vo. cloth, 4s. 6d.

II.

THE WATERING PLACES OF ENGLAND, CONSIDERED with Reference to their Medical Topography. Fourth Edition. Fcap. 8vo. cloth, 7s. 6d.

III.

THE BATHS OF GERMANY. Fourth Edition. Post 8vo. cloth, 7s.

IV.

HOMŒOPATHY AND HYDROPATHY IMPARTIALLY APPRECIATED. With Notes illustrative of the Influence of the Mind over the Body. Fourth Edition. Post 8vo. cloth, 3s. 6d.

MR. HENRY LEE, F.R.C.S.

ON SYPHILIS. Second Edition. With Coloured Plates. 8vo. cloth, 10s.

DR. ROBERT LEE, F.R.S.

I.

CONSULTATIONS IN MIDWIFERY. Foolscap 8vo. cloth, 4s. 6d.

II.

A TREATISE ON THE SPECULUM; with Three Hundred Cases. 8vo. cloth, 4s. 6d.

III.

CLINICAL REPORTS OF OVARIAN AND UTERINE DISEASES, with Commentaries. Foolscap 8vo. cloth, 6s. 6d.

IV.

CLINICAL MIDWIFERY: comprising the Histories of 545 Cases of Difficult, Preternatural, and Complicated Labour, with Commentaries. Second Edition. Foolscap 8vo. cloth, 5s.

V.

PRACTICAL OBSERVATIONS ON DISEASES OF THE UTERUS. With coloured Plates. Two Parts. Imperial 4to., 7s. 6d. each Part.

DR. LEISHMAN, M.D., F.F.P.S.
THE MECHANISM OF PARTURITION: An Essay, Historical and Critical. With Engravings. 8vo. cloth, 5s.

MR. LISTON, F.R.S.
PRACTICAL SURGERY. Fourth Edition. 8vo. cloth, 22s.

MR. H. W. LOBB, L.S.A., M.R.C.S.E.
ON SOME OF THE MORE OBSCURE FORMS OF NERVOUS AFFECTIONS, THEIR PATHOLOGY AND TREATMENT. Re-issue, with the Chapter on Galvanism entirely Re-written. With Engravings. 8vo. cloth, 8s.

LONDON MEDICAL SOCIETY OF OBSERVATION.
WHAT TO OBSERVE AT THE BED-SIDE, AND AFTER DEATH. Published by Authority. Second Edition. Foolscap 8vo. cloth, 4s. 6d.

DR. MACKENZIE, M.D., M.R.C.P.
THE PATHOLOGY AND TREATMENT OF PHLEGMASIA DOLENS, as deduced from Clinical and Physiological Researches. Lettsomian Lectures on Midwifery. 8vo. cloth, 6s.

MR. M'CLELLAND, F.L.S., F.G.S.
THE MEDICAL TOPOGRAPHY, OR CLIMATE AND SOILS, OF BENGAL AND THE N. W. PROVINCES. Post 8vo. cloth, 4s. 6d.

DR. MACLACHLAN, M.D., F.R.C.P. LOND.
THE DISEASES AND INFIRMITIES OF ADVANCED LIFE. 8vo. cloth, 16s.

DR. GEORGE H. B. MACLEOD, F.R.C.S. (EDIN.)
NOTES ON THE SURGERY OF THE CRIMEAN WAR; with REMARKS on GUN-SHOT WOUNDS. 8vo. cloth, 10s. 6d.

MR. JOSEPH MACLISE, F.R.C.S.
I.
SURGICAL ANATOMY. A Series of Dissections, illustrating the Principal Regions of the Human Body.
The Second Edition, imperial folio, cloth, £3. 12s.; half-morocco, £4. 4s.

II.
ON DISLOCATIONS AND FRACTURES. This Work is Uniform with the Author's "Surgical Anatomy;" each Fasciculus contains Four beautifully executed Lithographic Drawings. Imperial folio, cloth, £2. 10s.; half-morocco, £2. 17s.

DR. MCNICOLL, M.R.C.P.
A HAND-BOOK FOR SOUTHPORT, MEDICAL & GENERAL; with Copious Notices of the Natural History of the District. Second Edition. Post 8vo. cloth, 3s. 6d.

DR. MARCET, F.R.S.
I.
ON THE COMPOSITION OF FOOD, AND HOW IT IS ADULTERATED; with Practical Directions for its Analysis. 8vo. cloth, 6s. 6d.

II.
ON CHRONIC ALCOHOLIC INTOXICATION; with an INQUIRY INTO THE INFLUENCE OF THE ABUSE OF ALCOHOL AS A PRE-DISPOSING CAUSE OF DISEASE. Second Edition, much enlarged. Foolscap 8vo. cloth, 4s. 6d.

DR. MARKHAM.

I.

DISEASES OF THE HEART: THEIR PATHOLOGY, DIAG-
NOSIS, AND TREATMENT. Second Edition. Post 8vo. cloth, 6s.

II.

SKODA ON AUSCULTATION AND PERCUSSION. Post 8vo.
cloth, 6s.

SIR RANALD MARTIN, K.C.B., F.R.S.

INFLUENCE OF TROPICAL CLIMATES IN PRODUCING
THE ACUTE ENDEMIC DISEASES OF EUROPEANS; including Practical
Observations on their Chronic Sequelæ under the Influences of the Climate of Europe.
Second Edition, much enlarged. 8vo. cloth, 20s.

DR. MASSY.

ON THE EXAMINATION OF RECRUITS; intended for the Use of
Young Medical Officers on Entering the Army. 8vo. cloth, 5s.

MR. C. F. MAUNDER, F.R.C.S.

OPERATIVE SURGERY. With 158 Engravings. Post 8vo. 6s.

DR. MAYNE.

I.

AN EXPOSITORY LEXICON OF THE TERMS, ANCIENT
AND MODERN, IN MEDICAL AND GENERAL SCIENCE, including a complete MEDICAL AND MEDICO-LEGAL VOCABULARY. Complete in 10 Parts,
price 5s. each. The entire work, cloth, £2. 10s.

II.

A MEDICAL VOCABULARY; or, an Explanation of all Names,
Synonymes, Terms, and Phrases used in Medicine and the relative branches of Medical
Science, intended specially as a Book of Reference for the Young Student. Second
Edition. Fcap. 8vo. cloth, 8s. 6d.

DR. MILLINGEN.

ON THE TREATMENT AND MANAGEMENT OF THE IN-
SANE; with Considerations on Public and Private Lunatic Asylums. 18mo. cloth,
4s. 6d.

DR. W. J. MOORE, M.D.

I.

HEALTH IN THE TROPICS; or, Sanitary Art applied to Europeans
in India. 8vo. cloth, 9s.

II.

A MANUAL OF THE DISEASES OF INDIA. Fcap. 8vo. cloth, 5s.

PROFESSOR MULDER, UTRECHT.

THE CHEMISTRY OF WINE. Edited by H. BENCE JONES, M.D.,
F.R.S. Fcap. 8vo. cloth, 6s.

DR. BIRKBECK NEVINS.

THE PRESCRIBER'S ANALYSIS OF THE BRITISH PHAR-
MACOPEIA. 32mo. cloth, 2s. 6d.

DR. NOBLE.
THE HUMAN MIND IN ITS RELATIONS WITH THE
BRAIN AND NERVOUS SYSTEM. Post 8vo. cloth, 4s. 6d.

MR. NUNNELEY, F.R.C.S.E.
I.
ON THE ORGANS OF VISION: THEIR ANATOMY AND PHYSIOLOGY. With Plates, 8vo. cloth, 15s.
II.
A TREATISE ON THE NATURE, CAUSES, AND TREATMENT
OF ERYSIPELAS. 8vo. cloth, 10s. 6d.

DR. O'REILLY.
THE PLACENTA, THE ORGANIC NERVOUS SYSTEM,
THE BLOOD, THE OXYGEN, AND THE ANIMAL NERVOUS SYSTEM, PHYSIOLOGICALLY EXAMINED. With Engravings. 8vo. cloth, 5s.

MR. LANGSTON PARKER.
THE MODERN TREATMENT OF SYPHILITIC DISEASES,
both Primary and Secondary; comprising the Treatment of Constitutional and Confirmed Syphilis, by a safe and successful Method. Fourth Edition, 8vo. cloth, 10s.

DR. PARKES, F.R.C.P.
THE URINE: ITS COMPOSITION IN HEALTH AND DISEASE,
AND UNDER THE ACTION OF REMEDIES. 8vo. cloth, 12s.

DR. PARKIN, M.D., F.R.C.S.
THE CAUSATION AND PREVENTION OF DISEASE with
the Laws regulating the Extrication of Malaria from the Surface, and its Diffusion in the surrounding Air. 8vo. cloth, 5s.

MR. JAMES PART, F.R.C.S.
THE MEDICAL AND SURGICAL POCKET CASE BOOK,
for the Registration of important Cases in Private Practice, and to assist the Student of Hospital Practice. Second Edition. 2s. 6d.

DR. PAVY, M.D., F.R.S., F.R.C.P.
DIABETES : RESEARCHES ON ITS NATURE AND TREATMENT. 8vo. cloth, 8s. 6d.

DR. THOMAS B. PEACOCK, M.D.
ON THE INFLUENZA, OR EPIDEMIC CATARRHAL FEVER
OF 1847-8. 8vo. cloth, 5s. 6d.

DR. PEREIRA, F.R.S.
SELECTA E PRÆSCRIPTIS : with a Key, containing the Prescriptions
in an Unabbreviated Form, and a Literal Translation. Thirteenth Edition. 24mo. cloth, 5s.

DR. PICKFORD.
HYGIENE; or, Health as Depending upon the Conditions of the Atmosphere, Food and Drinks, Motion and Rest, Sleep and Wakefulness, Secretions, Excretions, and Retentions, Mental Emotions, Clothing, Bathing, &c. Vol. I. 8vo. cloth, 9s.

MR. PIRRIE, F.R.S.E.

THE PRINCIPLES AND PRACTICE OF SURGERY. With numerous Engravings on Wood. Second Edition. 8vo. cloth, 24s.

PHARMACOPŒIA COLLEGII REGALIS MEDICORUM LONDINENSIS. 8vo. cloth, 9s.; or 24mo. 5s.

IMPRIMATUR.

Hic liber, cui titulus, PHARMACOPŒIA COLLEGII REGALIS MEDICORUM LONDINENSIS. Datum ex Ædibus Collegii in comitiis censoriis, Novembris Mensis 14to 1850.

JOHANNES AYRTON PARIS. *Præses.*

PROFESSORS PLATTNER & MUSPRATT.

THE USE OF THE BLOWPIPE IN THE EXAMINATION OF MINERALS, ORES, AND OTHER METALLIC COMBINATIONS. Illustrated by numerous Engravings on Wood. Third Edition. 8vo. cloth, 10s. 6d.

DR. HENRY F. A. PRATT, M.D., M.R.C.P.

I.

THE GENEALOGY OF CREATION, newly Translated from the Unpointed Hebrew Text of the Book of Genesis, showing the General Scientific Accuracy of the Cosmogony of Moses and the Philosophy of Creation. 8vo. cloth, 14s.

II.

ON ECCENTRIC AND CENTRIC FORCE: A New Theory of Projection. With Engravings. 8vo. cloth, 10s.

III.

ON ORBITAL MOTION: The Outlines of a System of Physical Astronomy. With Diagrams. 8vo. cloth, 7s. 6d.

THE PRESCRIBER'S PHARMACOPŒIA; containing all the Medicines in the British Pharmacopœia, arranged in Classes according to their Action, with their Composition and Doses. By a Practising Physician. Fifth Edition. 32mo. cloth, 2s. 6d.; roan tuck (for the pocket), 3s. 6d.

DR. JOHN ROWLISON PRETTY.

AIDS DURING LABOUR, including the Administration of Chloroform, the Management of Placenta and Post-partum Hæmorrhage. Fcap. 8vo. cloth, 4s. 6d.

MR. LAKE PRICE.

PHOTOGRAPHIC MANIPULATION: Treating of the Practice of the Art, and its various appliances to Nature. With Fifty Engravings on Wood. Post 8vo. cloth, 6s. 6d.

MR. P. C. PRICE, F.R.C.S.E.

I.

SCROFULOUS DISEASES OF THE EXTERNAL LYMPHATIC GLANDS: their Nature, Variety, and Treatment; with Remarks on the Management of Scrofulous Ulcerations, Scars, and Cicatrices. Post 8vo. cloth, 3s. 6d.

II.

THE WINTER CLIMATE OF MENTON, WITH HINTS TO INVALIDS INTENDING TO RESIDE THERE. Fcap. 8vo. cloth, 3s.

DR. PRIESTLEY.

LECTURES ON THE DEVELOPMENT OF THE GRAVID UTERUS. 8vo. cloth, 5s. 6d.

DR. RADCLIFFE, F.R.C.P. LOND.
ON EPILEPTIC AND OTHER CONVULSIVE AFFECTIONS
OF THE NERVOUS SYSTEM. Third Edition. Post 8vo. cloth, 7s. 6d.

MR. RAINEY.
ON THE MODE OF FORMATION OF SHELLS OF ANIMALS,
OF BONE, AND OF SEVERAL OTHER STRUCTURES, by a Process of Molecular Coalescence, Demonstrable in certain Artificially-formed Products. Fcap. 8vo. cloth, 4s. 6d.

DR. F. H. RAMSBOTHAM.
THE PRINCIPLES AND PRACTICE OF OBSTETRIC MEDI-
CINE AND SURGERY. Illustrated with One Hundred and Twenty Plates on Steel and Wood; forming one thick handsome volume. Fourth Edition. 8vo. cloth, 22s.

DR. RAMSBOTHAM.
PRACTICAL OBSERVATIONS ON MIDWIFERY, with a Selection
of Cases. Second Edition. 8vo. cloth, 12s.

PROFESSOR REDWOOD, PH.D.
A SUPPLEMENT TO THE PHARMACOPŒIA: A concise but
comprehensive Dispensatory, and Manual of Facts and Formulæ, for the use of Practitioners in Medicine and Pharmacy. Third Edition. 8vo. cloth, 22s.

DR. DU BOIS REYMOND.
ANIMAL ELECTRICITY; Edited by H. BENCE JONES, M.D., F.R.S.
With Fifty Engravings on Wood. Foolscap 8vo. cloth, 6s.

DR. REYNOLDS, M.D. LOND.
I.
EPILEPSY: ITS SYMPTOMS, TREATMENT, AND RELATION
TO OTHER CHRONIC CONVULSIVE DISEASES. 8vo. cloth, 10s.
II.
THE DIAGNOSIS OF DISEASES OF THE BRAIN, SPINAL
CORD, AND THEIR APPENDAGES. 8vo. cloth, 8s.

DR. B. W. RICHARDSON.
I.
ON THE CAUSE OF THE COAGULATION OF THE BLOOD.
Being the ASTLEY COOPER PRIZE ESSAY for 1856. With a Practical Appendix. 8vo. cloth, 16s.
II.
THE HYGIENIC TREATMENT OF PULMONARY CONSUMP-
TION. 8vo. cloth, 5s. 6d.
III.
THE ASCLEPIAD. Vol. I., Clinical Essays. 8vo. cloth, 6s. 6d.

MR. WILLIAM ROBERTS.
AN ESSAY ON WASTING PALSY; being a Systematic Treatise on
the Disease hitherto described as ATROPHIE MUSCULAIRE PROGRESSIVE. With Four Plates. 8vo. cloth, 7s. 6d.

DR. ROUTH.
INFANT FEEDING, AND ITS INFLUENCE ON LIFE;
Or, the Causes and Prevention of Infant Mortality. Second Edition. Fcap. 8vo. cloth, 6s.

DR. W. H. ROBERTSON.

I.

THE NATURE AND TREATMENT OF GOUT.
8vo. cloth, 10s. 6d.

II.

A TREATISE ON DIET AND REGIMEN.
Fourth Edition. 2 vols. post 8vo. cloth, 12s.

DR. ROWE.

NERVOUS DISEASES, LIVER AND STOMACH COM-
PLAINTS, LOW SPIRITS, INDIGESTION, GOUT, ASTHMA, AND DIS-
ORDERS PRODUCED BY TROPICAL CLIMATES. With Cases. Sixteenth
Edition. Fcap. 8vo. 2s. 6d.

DR. ROYLE, F.R.S., AND DR. HEADLAND, M.D.

A MANUAL OF MATERIA MEDICA AND THERAPEUTICS.
With numerous Engravings on Wood. Third Edition. Fcap. 8vo. cloth, 12s. 6d.

MR. RUMSEY, F.R.C.S.

ESSAYS ON STATE MEDICINE. 8vo. cloth, 10s. 6d.

DR. RYAN, M.D.

INFANTICIDE: ITS LAW, PREVALENCE, PREVENTION, AND
HISTORY. 8vo. cloth, 5s.

ST. BARTHOLOMEW'S HOSPITAL.

A DESCRIPTIVE CATALOGUE OF THE ANATOMICAL
MUSEUM. Vol. I. (1846), Vol. II. (1851), Vol. III. (1862), 8vo. cloth, 5s. each.

DR. SALTER, F.R.S.

ON ASTHMA: its Pathology, Causes, Consequences, and Treatment.
8vo. cloth, 10s.

DR. SAVAGE, M.D. LOND., F.R.C.S.

THE SURGERY OF THE FEMALE PELVIC ORGANS, in
a Series of Plates taken from Nature, with Physiological and Pathological References.
Royal 4to. cloth, 20s.
. These Plates give 40 Illustrations taken from original Dissections, and are drawn
and coloured in the highest degree of art.

MR. SAVORY.

A COMPENDIUM OF DOMESTIC MEDICINE, AND COMPA-
NION TO THE MEDICINE CHEST; intended as a Source of Easy Reference for
Clergymen, and for Families residing at a Distance from Professional Assistance.
Sixth Edition. 12mo. cloth, 5s.

DR. SCHACHT.

THE MICROSCOPE, AND ITS APPLICATION TO VEGETABLE
ANATOMY AND PHYSIOLOGY. Edited by FREDERICK CURREY, M.A. Fcap.
8vo. cloth, 6s.

DR. SCORESBY-JACKSON, M.D., F.R.S.E.

MEDICAL CLIMATOLOGY; or, a Topographical and Meteorological
Description of the Localities resorted to in Winter and Summer by Invalids of various
classes both at Home and Abroad. With an Isothermal Chart. Post 8vo. cloth, 12s.

DR. SEMPLE.

ON COUGH: its Causes, Varieties, and Treatment. With some practical
Remarks on the Use of the Stethoscope as an aid to Diagnosis. Post 8vo. cloth, 4s. 6d.

DR. SEYMOUR.

I.

ILLUSTRATIONS OF SOME OF THE PRINCIPAL DIS-
EASES OF THE OVARIA: their Symptoms and Treatment; to which are prefixed Observations on the Structure and Functions of those parts in the Human Being and in Animals. With 14 folio plates, 12s.

II.

THE NATURE AND TREATMENT OF DROPSY ; considered
especially in reference to the Diseases of the Internal Organs of the Body, which most commonly produce it. 8vo. 5s.

DR. SHAPTER, M.D., F.R.C.P.

THE CLIMATE OF THE SOUTH OF DEVON, AND ITS
INFLUENCE UPON HEALTH. Second Edition, with Maps. 8vo. cloth, 10s. 6d.

MR. SHAW, M.R.C.S.

THE MEDICAL REMEMBRANCER ; OR, BOOK OF EMER-
GENCIES: in which are concisely pointed out the Immediate Remedies to be adopted in the First Moments of Danger from Drowning, Poisoning, Apoplexy, Burns, and other Accidents; with the Tests for the Principal Poisons, and other useful Information. Fourth Edition. Edited, with Additions, by JONATHAN HUTCHINSON, F.R.C.S. 32mo. cloth, 2s. 6d.

DR. SHEA, M.D., B.A.

A MANUAL OF ANIMAL PHYSIOLOGY. With an Appendix of
Questions for the B.A. London and other Examinations. With Engravings. Foolscap 8vo. cloth, 5s. 6d.

DR. SIBSON, F.R.S.

MEDICAL ANATOMY. With coloured Plates. Imperial folio. Fasci-
culi I. to VI. 5s. each.

DR. E. H. SIEVEKING.

ON EPILEPSY AND EPILEPTIFORM SEIZURES: their
Causes, Pathology, and Treatment. Second Edition. Post 8vo. cloth, 10s. 6d.

MR. SINCLAIR AND DR. JOHNSTON.

PRACTICAL MIDWIFERY : Comprising an Account of 13,748 Deli-
veries, which occurred in the Dublin Lying-in Hospital, during a period of Seven Years. 8vo. cloth, 15s.

DR. SIORDET, M.B. LOND., M.R.C.P.

MENTONE IN ITS MEDICAL ASPECT. Foolscap 8vo. cloth, 2s. 6d.

MR. ALFRED SMEE, F.R.S.

GENERAL DEBILITY AND DEFECTIVE NUTRITION ; their
Causes, Consequences, and Treatment. Second Edition. Fcap. 8vo. cloth, 3s. 6d.

DR. SMELLIE.

OBSTETRIC PLATES: being a Selection from the more Important and
Practical Illustrations contained in the Original Work. With Anatomical and Practical Directions. 8vo. cloth, 5s.

MR. HENRY SMITH, F.R.C.S.

I.

ON STRICTURE OF THE URETHRA. 8vo. cloth, 7s. 6d.

II.

HÆMORRHOIDS AND PROLAPSUS OF THE RECTUM :
Their Pathology and Treatment, with especial reference to the use of Nitric Acid. Third Edition. Fcap. 8vo. cloth, 3s.

DR. W. TYLER SMITH.

I.

A MANUAL OF OBSTETRICS, THEORETICAL AND PRAC-
TICAL. Illustrated with 186 Engravings. Fcap. 8vo. cloth, 12s. 6d.

II.

THE PATHOLOGY AND TREATMENT OF LEUCORRHŒA.
With Engravings on Wood. 8vo. cloth, 7s.

DR. SNOW.

ON CHLOROFORM AND OTHER ANÆSTHETICS: THEIR
ACTION AND ADMINISTRATION. Edited, with a Memoir of the Author, by
Benjamin W. Richardson, M.D. 8vo. cloth, 10s. 6d.

DR. STANHOPE TEMPLEMAN SPEER.

PATHOLOGICAL CHEMISTRY, IN ITS APPLICATION TO
THE PRACTICE OF MEDICINE. Translated from the French of MM. BECQUEREL
and RODIER. 8vo. cloth, reduced to 8s.

MR. PETER SQUIRE.

THE PHARMACOPÆIAS OF THIRTEEN OF THE LONDON
HOSPITALS, arranged in Groups for easy Reference and Comparison. 18mo. cloth,
3s. 6d.

DR. STEGGALL.

STUDENTS' BOOKS FOR EXAMINATION.

I.

A MEDICAL MANUAL FOR APOTHECARIES' HALL AND OTHER MEDICAL
BOARDS. Twelfth Edition. 12mo. cloth, 10s.

II.

A MANUAL FOR THE COLLEGE OF SURGEONS; intended for the Use
of Candidates for Examination and Practitioners. Second Edition. 12mo. cloth, 10s.

III.

GREGORY'S CONSPECTUS MEDICINÆ THEORETICÆ. The First Part, con-
taining the Original Text, with an Ordo Verborum, and Literal Translation. 12mo.
cloth, 10s.

IV.

THE FIRST FOUR BOOKS OF CELSUS; containing the Text, Ordo Verb-
orum, and Translation. Second Edition. 12mo. cloth, 8s.

V.

FIRST LINES FOR CHEMISTS AND DRUGGISTS PREPARING FOR EX-
AMINATION AT THE PHARMACEUTICAL SOCIETY. Second Edition.
18mo. cloth, 3s. 6d.

MR. STOWE, M.R.C.S.

A TOXICOLOGICAL CHART, exhibiting at one view the Symptoms,
Treatment, and Mode of Detecting the various Poisons, Mineral, Vegetable, and Animal.
To which are added, concise Directions for the Treatment of Suspended Animation.
Twelfth Edition, revised. On Sheet, 2s.; mounted on Roller, 5s.

MR. FRANCIS SUTTON, F.C.S.

A SYSTEMATIC HANDBOOK OF VOLUMETRIC ANALYSIS;
or, the Quantitative Estimation of Chemical Substances by Measure. With Engravings.
Post 8vo. cloth, 7s. 6d.

DR. SWAYNE.

OBSTETRIC APHORISMS FOR THE USE OF STUDENTS
COMMENCING MIDWIFERY PRACTICE. With Engravings on Wood. Third
Edition. Fcap. 8vo. cloth, 3s. 6d.

MR. TAMPLIN, F.R.C.S.E.

LATERAL CURVATURE OF THE SPINE: its Causes, Nature, and
Treatment. 8vo. cloth, 4s.

DR. ALEXANDER TAYLOR, F.R.S.E.

THE CLIMATE OF PAU; with a Description of the Watering Places
of the Pyrenees, and of the Virtues of their respective Mineral Sources in Disease. Third
Edition. Post 8vo. cloth, 7s.

DR. ALFRED S. TAYLOR, F.R.S.
I.
A MANUAL OF MEDICAL JURISPRUDENCE. Seventh Edition.
Fcap. 8vo. cloth, 12s. 6d.
II.
ON POISONS, in relation to MEDICAL JURISPRUDENCE AND
MEDICINE. Second Edition. Fcap. 8vo. cloth, 12s. 6d.

MR. TEALE.

ON AMPUTATION BY A LONG AND A SHORT RECTAN-
GULAR FLAP. With Engravings on Wood. 8vo. cloth, 5s.

DR. THEOPHILUS THOMPSON, F.R.S.

CLINICAL LECTURES ON PULMONARY CONSUMPTION;
with additional Chapters by E. SYMES THOMPSON, M.D. With Plates. 8vo. cloth, 7s. 6d.

DR. THOMAS.

THE MODERN PRACTICE OF PHYSIC; exhibiting the Symp-
toms, Causes, Morbid Appearances, and Treatment of the Diseases of all Climates.
Eleventh Edition. Revised by ALGERNON FRAMPTON, M.D. 2 vols. 8vo. cloth, 28s.

MR. HENRY THOMPSON, F.R.C.S.
I.
STRICTURE OF THE URETHRA; its Pathology and Treatment.
The Jacksonian Prize Essay for 1852. With Plates. Second Edition. 8vo. cloth, 10s.
II.
THE DISEASES OF THE PROSTATE; their Pathology and Treat-
ment. Comprising a Dissertation "On the Healthy and Morbid Anatomy of the Prostate
Gland;" being the Jacksonian Prize Essay for 1860. With Plates. Second Edition.
8vo. cloth, 10s.
III.
PRACTICAL LITHOTOMY AND LITHOTRITY; or, An Inquiry
into the best Modes of removing Stone from the Bladder. With numerous Engravings,
8vo. cloth, 9s.

DR. THUDICHUM.
I.
A TREATISE ON THE PATHOLOGY OF THE URINE,
Including a complete Guide to its Analysis. With Plates, 8vo. cloth, 14s.
II.
A TREATISE ON GALL STONES: their Chemistry, Pathology,
and Treatment. With Coloured Plates. 8vo. cloth, 10s.

DR. TILT.

I.

ON UTERINE AND OVARIAN INFLAMMATION, AND ON THE PHYSIOLOGY AND DISEASES OF MENSTRUATION. Third Edition. 8vo. cloth, 12s.

II.

A HANDBOOK OF UTERINE THERAPEUTICS. Post 8vo. cloth, 6s.

III.

THE CHANGE OF LIFE IN HEALTH AND DISEASE: a
Practical Treatise on the Nervous and other Affections incidental to Women at the Decline of Life. Second Edition. 8vo. cloth, 6s.

DR. GODWIN TIMMS.

CONSUMPTION: its True Nature and Successful Treatment. Crown 8vo. cloth, 10s.

DR. ROBERT B. TODD, F.R.S.

I.

CLINICAL LECTURES ON THE PRACTICE OF MEDICINE.
New Edition, in one Volume, Edited by Dr. BEALE, 8vo. cloth, 18s.

II.

ON CERTAIN DISEASES OF THE URINARY ORGANS, AND ON DROPSIES. Fcap. 8vo. cloth, 6s.

MR. TOMES, F.R.S.

A MANUAL OF DENTAL SURGERY. With 208 Engravings on Wood. Fcap. 8vo. cloth, 12s. 6d.

MR. JOSEPH TOYNBEE, F.R.S., F.R.C.S.

THE DISEASES OF THE EAR: THEIR NATURE, DIAGNOSIS, AND TREATMENT. Illustrated with numerous Engravings on Wood. 8vo. cloth, 15s.

DR. TURNBULL.

I.

AN INQUIRY INTO THE CURABILITY OF CONSUMPTION, ITS PREVENTION, AND THE PROGRESS OF IMPROVEMENT IN THE TREATMENT. Third Edition. 8vo. cloth, 6s.

II.

A PRACTICAL TREATISE ON DISORDERS OF THE STOMACH
with FERMENTATION; and on the Causes and Treatment of Indigestion, &c. 8vo. cloth, 6s.

DR. TWEEDIE, F.R.S.

CONTINUED FEVERS: THEIR DISTINCTIVE CHARACTERS, PATHOLOGY, AND TREATMENT. With Coloured Plates. 8vo. cloth, 12s.

VESTIGES OF THE NATURAL HISTORY OF CREATION.
Eleventh Edition. Illustrated with 106 Engravings on Wood. 8vo. cloth, 7s. 6d.

DR. UNDERWOOD.
TREATISE ON THE DISEASES OF CHILDREN. Tenth Edition, with Additions and Corrections by HENRY DAVIES, M.D. 8vo. cloth, 15s.

DR. UNGER.
BOTANICAL LETTERS. Translated by Dr. B. PAUL. Numerous Woodcuts. Post 8vo., 2s. 6d.

MR. WADE, F.R.C.S.
STRICTURE OF THE URETHRA. ITS COMPLICATIONS AND EFFECTS; a Practical Treatise on the Nature and Treatment of those Affections. Fourth Edition. 8vo. cloth, 7s. 6d.

DR. WALLER.
ELEMENTS OF PRACTICAL MIDWIFERY; or, Companion to the Lying-in Room. Fourth Edition, with Plates. Fcap. cloth, 4s. 6d.

MR. HAYNES WALTON, F.R.C.S.
SURGICAL DISEASES OF THE EYE. With Engravings on Wood. Second Edition. 8vo. cloth, 14s.

DR. WATERS, M.R.C.P.
I.
THE ANATOMY OF THE HUMAN LUNG. The Prize Essay to which the Fothergillian Gold Medal was awarded by the Medical Society of London. Post 8vo. cloth, 6s. 6d.
II.
RESEARCHES ON THE NATURE, PATHOLOGY, AND TREATMENT OF EMPHYSEMA OF THE LUNGS, AND ITS RELATIONS WITH OTHER DISEASES OF THE CHEST. With Engravings. 8vo. cloth, 5s.

DR. EBEN. WATSON, A.M.
ON THE TOPICAL MEDICATION OF THE LARYNX IN CERTAIN DISEASES OF THE RESPIRATORY AND VOCAL ORGANS. 8vo. cloth, 5s.

DR. ALLAN WEBB, F.R.C.S.L.
THE SURGEON'S READY RULES FOR OPERATIONS IN SURGERY. Royal 8vo. cloth, 10s. 6d.

DR. WEBER.
A CLINICAL HAND-BOOK OF AUSCULTATION AND PERCUSSION. Translated by JOHN COCKLE, M.D. 5s.

MR. SOELBERG WELLS, M.D., M.R.C.S.
ON LONG, SHORT, AND WEAK SIGHT, and their Treatment by the Scientific Use of Spectacles. With Engravings on Wood and Stone. 8vo. cloth, 5s.

MR. T. SPENCER WELLS, F.R.C.S.

I.

PRACTICAL OBSERVATIONS ON GOUT AND ITS COMPLI-
CATIONS, and on the Treatment of Joints Stiffened by Gouty Deposits. Foolscap 8vo. cloth, 5s.

II.

SCALE OF MEDICINES WITH WHICH MERCHANT VES-
SELS ARE TO BE FURNISHED, by command of the Privy Council for Trade; With Observations on the Means of Preserving the Health of Seamen, &c. &c. Seventh Thousand. Fcap. 8vo. cloth, 3s. 6d.

DR. WEST.

LECTURES ON THE DISEASES OF WOMEN. Second Edition.
8vo. cloth, 16s.

DR. UVEDALE WEST.

ILLUSTRATIONS OF PUERPERAL DISEASES. Second Edi-
tion, enlarged. Post 8vo. cloth, 5s.

MR. WHEELER.

HAND-BOOK OF ANATOMY FOR STUDENTS OF THE
FINE ARTS. With Engravings on Wood. Fcap. 8vo., 2s. 6d.

DR. WHITEHEAD, F.R.C.S.

ON THE TRANSMISSION FROM PARENT TO OFFSPRING
OF SOME FORMS OF DISEASE, AND OF MORBID TAINTS AND TENDENCIES. Second Edition. 8vo. cloth, 10s. 6d.

DR. WILLIAMS, F.R.S.

PRINCIPLES OF MEDICINE : An Elementary View of the Causes,
Nature, Treatment, Diagnosis, and Prognosis, of Disease. With brief Remarks on Hygienics, or the Preservation of Health. The Third Edition. 8vo. cloth, 15s.

THE WIFE'S DOMAIN : the YOUNG COUPLE—the MOTHER—the NURSE
—the NURSLING. Post 8vo. cloth, 3s. 6d.

DR. J. HUME WILLIAMS.

UNSOUNDNESS OF MIND, IN ITS MEDICAL AND LEGAL
CONSIDERATIONS. 8vo. cloth, 7s. 6d.

DR. WILLIAMSON, SURGEON-MAJOR, 64TH REGIMENT.

I.

MILITARY SURGERY. With Plates. 8vo. cloth, 12s.

II.

NOTES ON THE WOUNDED FROM THE MUTINY IN
INDIA: with a Description of the Preparations of Gunshot Injuries contained in the Museum at Fort Pitt. With Lithographic Plates. 8vo. cloth, 12s.

MR. ERASMUS WILSON, F.R.S.

I.

THE ANATOMIST'S VADE-MECUM: A SYSTEM OF HUMAN
ANATOMY. With numerous Illustrations on Wood. Eighth Edition. Foolscap 8vo. cloth, 12s. 6d.

II.

DISEASES OF THE SKIN: A Practical and Theoretical Treatise on
the DIAGNOSIS, PATHOLOGY, and TREATMENT OF CUTANEOUS DIS-EASES. Fifth Edition. 8vo. cloth, 16s.

THE SAME WORK; illustrated with finely executed Engravings on Steel, accurately coloured. 8vo. cloth, 34s.

III.

HEALTHY SKIN: A Treatise on the Management of the Skin and Hair
in relation to Health. Sixth Edition. Foolscap 8vo. 2s. 6d.

IV.

PORTRAITS OF DISEASES OF THE SKIN. Folio. Fasciculi I.
to XII., completing the Work. 20s. each. The Entire Work, half morocco, £13.

V.

ON SYPHILIS, CONSTITUTIONAL AND HEREDITARY;
AND ON SYPHILITIC ERUPTIONS. With Four Coloured Plates. 8vo. cloth, 16s.

VI.

A THREE WEEKS' SCAMPER THROUGH THE SPAS OF
GERMANY AND BELGIUM, with an Appendix on the Nature and Uses of Mineral Waters. Post 8vo. cloth, 6s. 6d.

VII.

THE EASTERN OR TURKISH BATH: its History, Revival in
Britain, and Application to the Purposes of Health. Foolscap 8vo., 2s.

DR. G. C. WITTSTEIN.
PRACTICAL PHARMACEUTICAL CHEMISTRY: An Explanation
of Chemical and Pharmaceutical Processes, with the Methods of Testing the Purity of the Preparations, deduced from Original Experiments. Translated from the Second German Edition, by STEPHEN DARBY. 18mo. cloth, 6s.

DR. HENRY G. WRIGHT.
HEADACHES; their Causes and their Cure. Third Edition. Fcap. 8vo.
2s. 6d.

DR. YEARSLEY, M.D., M.R.C.S.
I.

DEAFNESS PRACTICALLY ILLUSTRATED; being an Exposition
as to the Causes and Treatment of Diseases of the Ear. Sixth Edition. 8vo. cloth, 6s.

II.

ON THE ENLARGED TONSIL AND ELONGATED UVULA,
and other Morbid Conditions of the Throat. Seventh Edition. 8vo, cloth, 5s.

CHURCHILL'S SERIES OF MANUALS.

Fcap. 8vo. cloth, 12s. 6d. each.

"We here give Mr. Churchill public thanks for the positive benefit conferred on the Medical Profession, by the series of beautiful and cheap Manuals which bear his imprint."— *British and Foreign Medical Review.*

AGGREGATE SALE, 128,500 COPIES.

ANATOMY. With numerous Engravings. Eighth Edition. By ERASMUS WILSON, F.R.C.S., F.R.S.

BOTANY. With numerous Engravings. By ROBERT BENTLEY, F.L.S., Professor of Botany, King's College, and to the Pharmaceutical Society.

CHEMISTRY. With numerous Engravings. Ninth Edition. By GEORGE FOWNES, F.R.S., H. BENCE JONES, M.D., F.R.S., and A. W. HOFMANN, F.R.S.

DENTAL SURGERY. With numerous Engravings. By JOHN TOMES, F.R.S.

MATERIA MEDICA. With numerous Engravings. Third Edition. By J. FORBES ROYLE, M.D., F.R.S., and FREDERICK W. HEADLAND, M.D., F.L.S.

MEDICAL JURISPRUDENCE. Seventh Edition. By ALFRED SWAINE TAYLOR, M.D., F.R.S.

PRACTICE OF MEDICINE. Second Edition. By G. HILARO BARLOW, M.D., M.A.

The **MICROSCOPE and its REVELATIONS.** With numerous Plates and Engravings. Third Edition. By W. B. CARPENTER, M.D., F.R.S.

NATURAL PHILOSOPHY. With numerous Engravings. Fifth Edition. By GOLDING BIRD, M.D., M.A., F.R.S., and CHARLES BROOKE, M.B., M.A., F.R.S.

OBSTETRICS. With numerous Engravings. By W. TYLER SMITH, M.D., F.R.C.P.

OPHTHALMIC MEDICINE and SURGERY. With coloured Engravings on Steel, and Illustrations on Wood. Second Edition. By T. WHARTON JONES, F.R.C.S., F.R.S.

PATHOLOGICAL ANATOMY. With numerous Engravings. By C. HANDFIELD JONES, M.B., F.R.C.P., and E. H. SIEVEKING, M.D., F.R.C.P.

PHYSIOLOGY. With numerous Engravings. Third Edition. By WILLIAM B. CARPENTER, M.D., F.R.S.

POISONS. Second Edition. By ALFRED SWAINE TAYLOR, M.D., F.R.S.

PRACTICAL SURGERY. With numerous Engravings. Fourth Edition. By WILLIAM FERGUSSON, F.R.C.S.

Printed by W. BLANCHARD & SONS, 62, Millbank Street, Westminster.

www.ingramcontent.com/pod-product-compliance
Lightning Source LLC
Chambersburg PA
CBHW030603270326
41927CB00007B/1028